An Administrator's Garden

An Administrator's Garden

SOWING SEEDS OF HOPE

Cultivating a Church's Path to Greater
Achievement Through Seven Holistic
Life Skills

Mary J. Goodwin-Clinkscale, Th.D., C.Ed.D.

Foreword by Former Nebraska Congressman Lee Terry

©2019 Mary Goodwin-Clinkscale

All Rights Reserved. No part of this book may be used or reproduced by any means, graphic, electronic, or mechanical, including photocopying, recording, taping or by any information storage retrieval system without the express written permission of the publisher, except in the case of brief quotations embodied in critical articles and reviews.

Because of the dynamic nature of the internet, any web addresses or links contained in this book may have changed since publication and may no longer be valid. The views expressed in this work are solely those of the author and do not necessarily reflect the views of the publisher or their agents.

Disclaimers: Trademarks of products, services, and organizations mentioned herein belong to their respective owners and are not affiliated with the publisher.

Formal letters are printed with the express written permission of their authors.

Hardcover:	978-1-7342494-1-5
Paperback (color):	978-1-7342494-2-2
Paperback (b&w):	978-1-7342494-3-9
Kindle:	978-1-7342494-4-6

Library of Congress Cataloging Data on file with the publisher.

Printed in the United States of America.

10 9 8 7 6 5 4 3 2 1

"It is easier to build strong children than to repair broken men."

—Fredrick Douglass

AUTOGRAPHS

THIS BOOK BELONGS TO:

_____

End exceeds beginning.

—Ecclesiastes 7:8

Contents

LAST DAY	11
DEDICATION	13
ABOUT THE AUTHOR	19
BIOGRAPHY	20
INTRODUCTION	29
CHAPTER I: THE SKILL OF ADMINISTRATION	37
CHAPTER II: THE SKILL OF ORGANIZATION	67
CHAPTER III: THE SKILL OF LEADERSHIP	121
CHAPTER IV: THE SKILL OF LISTENING	141
CHAPTER V: THE SKILL OF COMMUNICATION	155
CHAPTER VI: THE SKILL OF MAKING YOUR PRESENTATION	169
CHAPTER VII: THE SKILL OF TEAMWORK	185
SUMMARY	197
PERSONAL REFLECTIONS	201
ACKNOWLEDGMENTS	205
THOUGHT EXPANSION	211
PHOTO GALLERY A	215
PHOTO GALLERY B	221
INSPIRATIONAL PASSAGES	241
AUTHOR PUBLICATIONS	243
SUGGESTED READINGS	245
INDEX	247
INDEX OF QUOTATIONS	251

"To the Creator and
Extender of
My Days"

"Life"

Last Day

The words "last" and "final" refer to what comes as an ending. That which is "last" comes or stands after all others in a stated series or succession. That which is "final" comes at the end, or serves to end or terminate… admitting of nothing further.

The word "day" is the interval of light between two successive nights. The portion of time allotted to work. A time considered favorable or opportune. A period of existence, power, or influence.

So, what are the words "last day?" In the aforementioned definitions, the words "last" and "day" could be combined to serve as a "final beginning." Final or last, meaning we have reached the pinnacle or crest of one's labor, culminating in completion. We have reached the "fullness" of an ending, yet… of a new beginning, starting with the next "day," which represents the process until completion. The development or progression of something is formed during the "day," the process before an ending. We reach the fullness of time for that process, and now, we are boarding a new "day" or new progression. Thus, "last day" is essentially reaching an "end to begin."

This is Dr. Mary J. Goodwin Clinkscale's "last day." She has reached an "end" and has now retired from former abundant labors. However, she is now embarking upon a new "day," a new beginning, a new quest… a quest to do even better. This book is a new quest, a new beginning, a new "day" for

Dr. Clinkscale to advance her journey of betterment. At this moment, the journey continues with you, the reader, who will now learn how to be a better planner, a better organizer, and a better administrator. Use what you learn throughout the pages of this book to help cultivate your administrative garden, and watch those seeds germinate, grow, and produce a fruitful and beautiful harvest from within your very own… "Administrator's Garden."

> ***This composition was inspired by my then seven-year-old grandson Ashton A. Goodwin who coined the phrase "Last day" for "Yesterday".***

Composed by his father
Darian L. Goodwin

Dedication

This book is dedicated to the memory of my beloved pastor, Bishop Dr. Nelson George Turner and his beautiful wife, Mother Hattie Pearl Turner, two people who I learned to love as my own family.

Through the teachings of the Word of God, these two taught me about life. They taught me by example how to live a better life, through exercising my God-given talents. I couldn't have ever imagined the vast and varied opportunities that have been afforded me, allowing me to hone and implement my diverse talents and skills.

Never had I heard a man speak like this man. The words that came from the pulpit were soothing to my soul, as a result of this message, I was adopted into the family of God. To God be the Glory, for the many blessings that continue to drive me onward and upward.

They were the catalysts who supported me as I expanded my innate talents within the walls of the church, and later the community. Because of this gift expansion, I could teach, direct, and implement the many productions, special functions and events that were orchestrated under their endorsement.

My thoughts—my continued motivation—to excel are furthered in remembrance of Bishop Dr. Turner, and Dr. Mother Turner; rest in peace knowing I love you both beyond all imagination.

FOREWORD A

Commemorative Letter to Dr. Mary J. Clinkscale from Former Nebraska Congressman Lee Terry
February 16, 2010

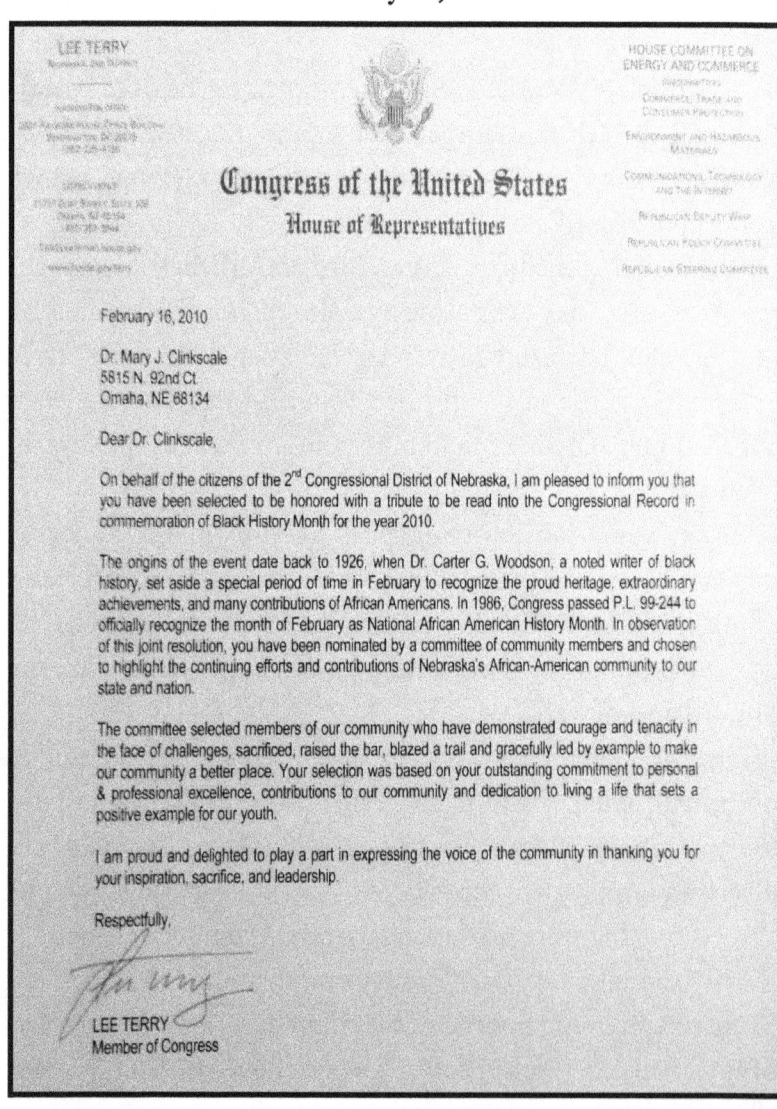

(TRANSCRIPTION OF FOREWORD A)

Dear Dr. Clinkscale,

On behalf of the citizens of the 2nd Congressional District of Nebraska, I am pleased to inform you that you have been selected to be honored with a tribute to be read into the Congressional Record in commemoration of Black History Month for the year 2010.

The origins of the event date back to 1926, when Dr. Carter G. Woodson, a noted writer of black history, set aside a special period in February to recognize the proud heritage, extraordinary achievements, and many contributions of African Americans. In 1986, Congress passed P.L. 99-244 to officially recognize the month of February as National African American History Month. In observation of this joint resolution, you have been nominated by a committee of community members and chosen to highlight the continuing efforts and contributions of Nebraska's African-American community to our state and nation.

The committee selected members of our community who have demonstrated courage and tenacity in the face of challenges, sacrificed, raised the bar, blazed a trail and gracefully led by example to make our community a **better** place. Your selection was based on your outstanding commitment to personal & professional excellence, contributions to our community and dedication to living a life that sets a positive example for our youth.

I am proud and delighted to play a part in expressing the voice of the community in thanking you for your inspiration, sacrifice, and leadership.

Respectfully,
LEE TERRY
Member of Congress

FOREWORD B

House of Representatives Tribute Read to Congress by Former Nebraska Congressman Lee Terry Honoring Dr. Mary J. Clinkscale
February 25, 2010

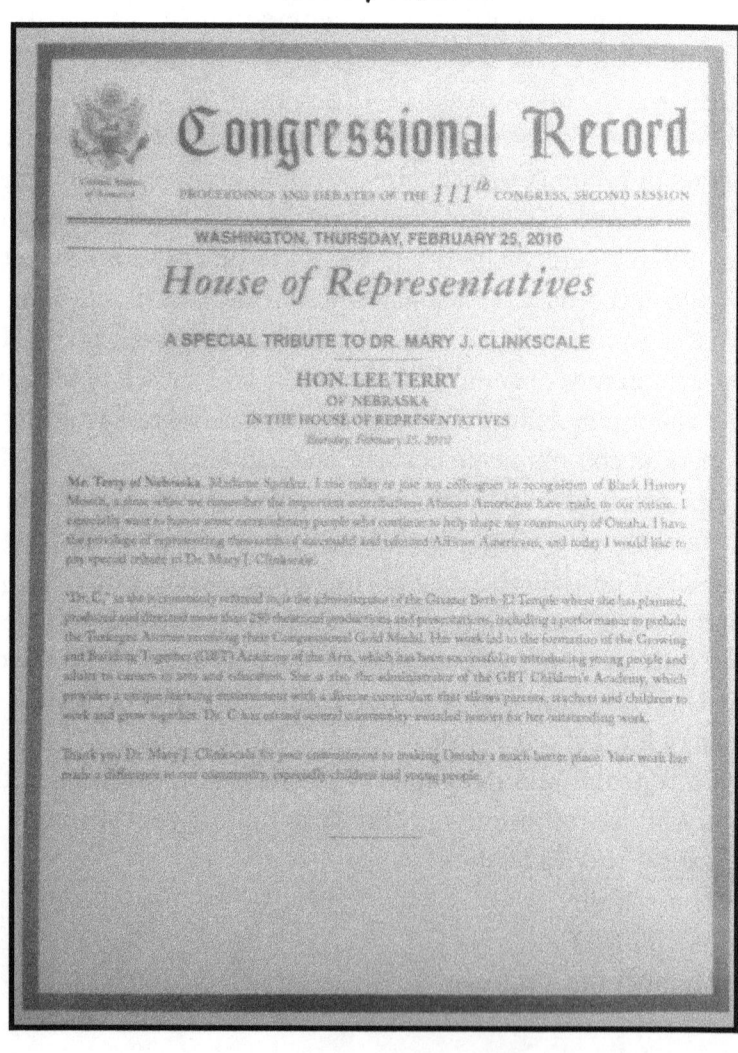

(TRANSCRIPTION OF FOREWORD B)

Mr. Terry of Nebraska.

Madame Speaker, I rise today to join my colleagues in recognition of Black History Month, a time when we remember the important contributions African Americans have made to our nation. I especially want to honor some extraordinary people who continue to help shape my community of Omaha. I have the privilege of representing thousands of successful and talented African Americans, and today I would like to pay special tribute to Dr. Mary J. Clinkscale.

"Dr. C," as she is commonly referred to, is the administrator of the Greater Beth-el Temple where she has planned, produced and directed more than 250 theatrical productions and presentations, including a performance to prelude the Tuskegee Airmen receiving their Congressional Gold Medal. Her work led to the formation of the GBT (Growing and Building Together) Academy of the Arts, which has been successful in introducing young people and adults to careers in arts and education. She is also the administrator of the GBT Children's Academy, which provides a unique learning environment with a diverse curriculum that allows parents, teachers and children to work and grow together. Dr. C has earned several community-awarded honors for her outstanding work.

Thank you, Dr. Mary J., Clinkscale for your commitment to making Omaha a much better place. Your work has made a difference to our community, especially children and young people.

MISSION OF THE GBT ACADEMY

"...to equip our youth with the character values of teamwork, discipline, respect, perseverance and leadership through diverse forms of artistic expression from the performing stage to the stage of life"

*Mission of GBT (Growing & Building Together)
Academy of the Arts (dissolved in 2013)*

Figure 1: "A Lone Wolf" painting by an amazing 8-year-old artist, Javon Bunch, GBTAA Student

About the Author

Former Administrator
Greater Beth-el Temple & GBT Children's Academy

Founder and Former Executive Producer/Director,
GBT (Growing and Building Together) Academy of the Arts

Founder & Former CEO
The Grand Barber and Beauty Salon

Dr. Mary J. Goodwin-Clinkscale (Dr. C) is a native of Conway County, Arkansas, born in the little town of Center Ridge (some 60 miles north of Little Rock), which at the time had a population of about 300. In the mid-1950's, she moved with her mother and extended family members to Omaha, Nebraska, where she currently resides. She is the mother of five sons, 16 grandchildren and six great-grandchildren.

Biography

Over 40 years ago, within the walls of Greater Beth-el Temple (formerly Greater Bethlehem Temple), Dr. C discovered her life's work. As the colors of life were revealed, she began to "paint." The more she "painted", the more color was added to her canvas. Her understanding of lessons learned from her life experiences increased as she unceasingly plowed in hope of better things to come. As God's providence continued to unfold, Dr. C desired to paint so others could capture the vision. She sought to share her knowledge with the community at large, beginning with the church family.

By using the Arts as a model for learning, this created a pattern for a higher standard of living. She saw people as God's works of art. As Dr. C reflects on the diverse perspectives and cultures that exist throughout our country, she states, "Do you see life in *black* and *white*, or do you see the richness of life in **color**?"

She has always felt that education was vital, not only as a personal goal, but to the success and growth of the church as well as the community. She has dedicated her life to carrying out this vision.

Dr. C's desire was to bring to life the spiritual messages that were taught in the church, and to portray their meaning in such a way as to make it easy to clearly understand what was communicated.

She indicates that her pastor embraced her use of these "non-traditional" methods of teaching through the visual and performing arts, which enriched lives and helped individuals of all ages to reach greater achievements.

Dr. Clinkscale served in numerous positions, both in the church and in the community, which contributed to her receiving the following degrees based, in part, on her life experiences:

Dr. C earned her Bachelor of Christian Education in Christian Fine Arts, Master of Arts in Administration and Organization, Doctorate Degree in Theology (Th. D) (*Distinguished Graduate*), and another in Christian Education in Administration and Organization (C. Ed. D.) (*Summa Cum Laude*), all from the International Apostolic University of Grace and Truth in Columbus, Ohio.

In the 1980s, she expanded her entrepreneurial wings by opening "Private Collections" by MJ, a specialty women's boutique, which offered a collection of unique women's apparel, neighboring her husband's barber shop, Hair Command. After six months, she decided to join her husband in the world of cosmetology, so she closed "Private Collections" and obtained her cosmetology license from Stewart's School of Cosmetology in 1993.

Together with her husband, David E. Goodwin Sr., she co-owned Hair Command Barber and Beauty Shop, which later became The Grand Barber and Beauty Salon. The Grand was a full-service salon which Dr. C owned and managed for 28 years, a combined total between the two businesses, before retiring in August 2013.

However, this was not her only retirement. After 40 years of dedicated service, Dr. C also retired from her duties as Vice President of The GBT Development Corporation; the Administrator of her church, Greater Beth-el Temple; the Administrator of GBT Children's Academy, which officially opened in 2008 and as the Producer/Director of GBT Academy of the Arts, which she'd begun (unofficially) in 1977. At this stage of her life, Dr. C states that she has retired from the external pressure and internal stress of working in these capacities, but her mind will never retire, as it is always entertaining new ideas. She is continuously looking for ways to incorporate those ideas. As she would say: "Life isn't over – just this chapter!"

The GBT Academy of the Arts evolved from a very simplistic beginning. During nearly 40 years at Greater Bethel Temple, Dr. C planned, produced and directed more than 300 programs and events including anniversaries, birthdays, holidays and other special occasions.

This was a performance and visual arts academy built on a strong educational background where the programs evolved into comprehensive, artistic productions. She brought in messages taken from what had been taught in the sanctuary, as well as current events, movies, and note-worthy news, and recast them in the form of live stage-plays. With the help and recruitment of many other dedicated individuals, she found entertainment to be a unique way of presenting common messages or ideas in unconventional ways.

The Academy's young people have been able to showcase their talents as well as develop a **better** understanding and appreciation for *the visual and the performing arts*. Through their participation in the performing arts, they have gained self-esteem and acquired many abilities to succeed personally and professionally. These skills include, but are not limited to accountability, creative thinking, problem-solving, leadership, communication, and teamwork.

Today, many of these individuals have entered professional fields including health, legal, human service and acting careers. Henceforth, the motto of the GBT Academy of the Arts, "From the performing stage to the stage of life."

Dr. C has fostered a new generation of leaders through her dynamic leadership and genuine interest in young people. Her lifelong commitment has provided high-quality performing arts education for individuals of all ages to express themselves, creating a venue for community entertainment and an appreciation for cultural diversity.

In addition to partnering with several nonprofit organizations for arts academy projects and performances, Dr. C served as the assistant director of the Greater Bethel Temple board, and director of the GBT Academy board. She also served on the Nebraska Arts Council Review Committee as part of a team that evaluated grant submissions. Other requests came from the community, such as serving on the Board of Directors with the University of Nebraska at Omaha Communications Department, and serving as an Assistant Convention Planning Coordinator for a national church organization. However, due to her demanding schedule and high commitment to GBT; she did not want to deviate from her prior commitments at that time.

Numerous awards and recognitions were received over the years through her involvement and service to her church including: Humanitarian Award, Bishop Dr. Nelson G. Turner Pillar of Excellence Award, Certificate of Appreciation (Directors Becoming Leaders; Leadership Development), Global Executor Extraordinaire, Dedicated Service Award (2), Overachiever Award, Distinguished Mentor, Superior Administrator, Ambitious Achiever, Business Woman of the Year, Professional Achievement, Award of Merit and Honor, Entrepreneur Award and Certificate of Appreciation for Devoted, Invaluable Services as Pastor's Aide Chairlady.

The pastor, Bishop Dr. Turner, often referred to this scripture when amplifying Dr. C.'s position as church administrator to the congregation.

> *I commend unto you Phebe our sister, which is a servant of the church which is at Cenchrea: That ye receive her in the Lord, as becometh saints, and that ye assist her in whatsoever business she hath need of you: for she hath been a succourer of many, and of myself also.*
>
> Romans 16:1, 2

In the late 20th century, the German-based chemical company Badische Anilin und Soda Fabrik (BASF), used as its marketing tagline: "We don't make a lot of the products you buy; we make a lot of the products you buy **better**." This is a resounding truth to the life of Dr. Mary J. Goodwin-Clinkscale, who has always recognized a need to do **better**, to make **better**, to live **better**; not only for herself, but for anyone or anything that needed improvement. Her story is one of development—of advancement—of **betterment**. Dr. C is always looking for ways to improve. She often states:

"Our best can always be better. Why settle for good when great can be had?"

PUBLIC AWARDS AND RECOGNITION RECEIVED (2007–PRESENT)

2015

- *Strathmore's Who's Who* for demonstrated leadership and achievement in her industry and profession.

2014

- **Birthday Celebration: Salute to 70 Years of Extended Life,** Guest Speaker and Author, Dr. Ronald W. Alston, Sr. Chicago, Illinois

2012

- *Veterans Support Award*, Metropolitan Community College, Office of Military and Veteran Support Services, Omaha, Nebraska
- *African-American Leadership Award (Community)*, Urban League of Nebraska
- *Certificate of Appreciation,* City of Los Angeles, California
- *County of Los Angeles Commendation*
- *California State Senate Certificate of Recognition*
- *Salute to Senior Service Award Nominee (received 27 letters of recognition),* Home Instead, Omaha, Nebraska

2011

- ***Syndicated Feature Story on National Fox News Channel Segment, "Beyond the Dream"*** – Presented by host and news anchor Kelly Wright in conjunction with a three-day fundraiser event for GBT Academy of the Arts, including renown guest speakers Dr. Bernard and Shirley Kinsey, of Pacific Palisades, California, and their son Khalil Kinsey, highlighting their historical African American art and artifacts, representing over 90 countries and six continents (www.thekinseycollection.com)

2010

- **2010 Black History Month Honoree– 2nd Congressional District of Nebraska**, presented by Congressman Lee Terry *(President Barack Obama, Oprah Winfrey, the late tennis champion Arthur Ash, and other renowned individuals received this same honor.)*

2009

- ***Exemplary Leadership Award***, GBT Academy of the Arts "Through the Fire" Fundraiser, University of Nebraska- Omaha (UNO)
- ***Women of Wisdom Award Nominee***, University of Nebraska-Omaha (UNO) Lifelong Learning Initiative

2008

- *Award of Appreciation*, Tuskegee Aviation Academy, Milwaukee, Wisconsin
- *Outstanding Citizen*, Woodmen of the World, Lodge 6124, Omaha, Nebraska
- *Woman of Distinction*, Midlands Business Journal, Omaha, Nebraska
- *Women of Color Award Recipient, Arts & Humanities*, University of Nebraska at Omaha

2007

- *Outstanding Recognition*, Tuskegee Airmen, Alphonso W. Davis Chapter, Omaha, Nebraska
- *Leota G. Norton Community Service Award*, United Way of the Midlands, Omaha, Nebraska
- *Heartland Blueprint Leadership Program Graduate*, United Way of the Midlands, Omaha, Nebraska (Presented commencement address)

Other Publicity and News Highlights

- Television: Fox National News channel,
- Channel 6 with Carol Schrader Omaha, Nebraska
- Channel 42 KPTM news Omaha, Nebraska
- Morning Blend Show Omaha, Nebraska
- WOWT 6 News Break with Jim Sidelecki, Omaha, Nebraska
- Newspaper: Omaha World-Herald, Bellevue Leader, Omaha Star, University of Nebraska Medical Center, Omaha Public Library, University of Nebraska at Omaha
- Magazine: The Reader, Midlands Business Journal, Omaha Magazine

Introduction

THE SEVEN LIFE SKILLS THAT REPRESENT COMPLETION

Seven is the number that represents completion (both naturally and spiritual). It derives much of its meaning from being tied directly to God's creation of all things. He created the world in six days and saw that his creation was good. On the seventh day, He rested from His creation. (Genesis 2:1-3) The notes on the music staff are organized into segments of 7 major notes each (C, D, E, F, G, A, B). The rays of visible light in the rainbow consist of seven distinct colors: red, green, violet, orange, indigo, yellow and blue. Days of the week on our calendar are organized after a natural seven-day progression.

You should strive always to work within the plan of God, as He has already laid the foundation, and the groundwork, for us to one day be made whole. Knowing this, should motivate you to start each day with purpose and perseverance to fulfill your *destiny*. Destiny means you are following a path for your life that has already been fore-ordained. It is also the power that is believed to determine the course of events. To acquire its benefits, you must listen carefully, put in the work, and organize your life around whatever it is you're seeking.

> *Just realize if it is to be, it is up to you!*

Many people have asked why it's important to be concerned with developing life skills. I believe there are many individuals who struggle with understanding and integrating life skills. We will focus on the following three questions:

- What are life skills?
- Why are life skills necessary?
- How can these skills be developed?

The Definition of Life Skills

Skills in general indicate the ability to do something well, and are gained by experience, through preparation, and practice, resulting in increased knowledge. Life skills lead people to better behaviors, that apply throughout their lives. They allow us to deal with the demands and challenges that ensue in handling problems that occur in everyday life.

Actively incorporating life skills enhances the process of organization, and more importantly, implementation in one's daily living. When cultivating a church's path to greater achievement, there are seven life skills that rise above all others in the way they have influenced my tenure in administration. I have selected these, as they not only have worked for me, but have also worked for many others over the years, including my very own family.

A "skill set" is the combination of abilities that connect to a job. One person may possess skills in different areas, however, he or she may be highly talented in some areas, of average talent in a few, and have underdeveloped skills in other areas of concern. Therefore, it is imperative that one identifies their strengths and weaknesses, to maximize their development and reach their full potential. Although I welcomed assistance from others in the compilation of this book, the ideas and information shared is from my own personal life experience, the use of my own personal life skills, and meticulous research, integrated with lessons learned through the School of Hard Knocks.

Life skills are necessary to live a richer, more fulfilling life. These abilities help organize all aspects of your life, from your personal well-being to your home, as well as your business or career, including church involvement. Enhancing your life skills will help to eliminate stress and increase available time to focus on other anticipated activities. *Work smarter, not harder.*

To develop life skills, one must be open to other ways of learning beyond the traditional classroom setting and be willing to move outside his comfort zone. It would be more beneficial if high school students could learn life skills during their primary school years. Students who receive life skills training beginning in their homes, have been shown to have a greater advantage over those who do not.

At the close of the day, *who* we become depends on *what* we learn. One's learning experience may come in several forms, including, but certainly not limited to:

- Interacting with people, listening attentively
- Listening to and learning new genres of music
- Volunteering one's services to the community
- Exposing oneself to other cultures
- Embracing diversity despite personal differences
- Traveling to various destinations
- Reading, Reading, Reading

> The greater your exposure,
> the broader your thinking.

Each of the seven life skills described in this publication were employed throughout the church environment and later implemented with the launch of the GBTAA nonprofit, community-based organization. These skills include administration, organization, leadership, listening, communication, making presentations, and teamwork. These skills are also applicable to any other organization or area of your life.

Using innovative and unconventional teaching methods, many individuals benefited from these opportunities for self-expression throughout our exercise of the visual and performing arts. In addition to the visual and performing arts presentations, various other activities in the church – such as the carry-out dinners – were planned and organized utilizing these skills. To perform effectively, those placed in leadership positions had to organize teams, and practice being effective communicators while exercising administrative roles. In most cases, the duties at hand required on-the-job training, even sometimes "baptism by fire."

Without utilizing these skills, the teams formed for each endeavor would not have been functional. The intended message conveyed through the result would not have been transparent. Regardless of the degree of one's experience, the learning possibilities are endless when one can embrace the talents of all involved. The secret here is to find who can do what, then place them in appropriate positions, which will make the outcome of the given project more meaningful.

We are born with God-given talents and abilities, but if they are not nurtured continuously, they begin to diminish. These abilities may be passed on to someone else.

A passage in the Bible describes the parable of the three servants who were given talents by their lord and how they used them. Two of the servants expanded their talents, while one hid his talent; and it was eventually taken away and given to the servant who had the most talents. (Matthew 25:14-30) Let us find ourselves nurturing the development of our innate talents and maximizing our impact not only in our own lives, but in the lives of others.

> "...every wise hearted man, in whom the Lord put wisdom and understanding to know how to work all manner of work for the service of the sanctuary..."
>
> Exodus 36:1

Throughout my career, I have been told, that I was hard and critical. While I accept this feedback, I would clarify that I was firm, but kind. My personal standard throughout the years has been to move with a mindset of excellence. Perfection was my goal; however, no one is perfect (faultless). Even so I had to know that no matter what level of effort and dedication I put into any project; the absolute best had to enter a carefully designed plan.

> "People say: 'Find good people and leave the bad ones.' But I say, 'find the good in people and ignore the bad in them. Because no one is perfect."
>
> Kenny Rogers

I would take this statement from Kenny Rogers a step further: you should then offer to help in the areas that need improvement. We should all strive to become matured.

Nothing happens unless you move to make it happen, and that should be sooner rather than later. When you procrastinate, you delay a process that has timelines and goals, which could affect promises you've made. However, it is never too late to start.

Sacrifice was one of the key elements to every successful mission upon which we embarked. To make these programs and events happen, my instruction, my leadership, and my examples placed me in front of the public eye. Therefore, the use of 'WE,' 'US,' 'OUR,' and 'LET'S,' became my words of choice.

> **When we change MY to OUR,**
> **I to US,**
> **ME to WE;**
> **we have UNITY.**

The confidence I shared with others was at the core of how we advanced, benefiting all who participated. Everyone I had been blessed to work with learned how important it was to magnify the combined efforts of the team. We patterned our behavior into a model to be perfected, as if God was always watching. When that exercise of 'Divine Intention' became the prime focus, success was never far behind.

Having an attitude or mindset of self-dignity and pride is deeply intertwined with the level of achievement and successful outcomes you reach in life. Your attitude of mind dictates your lifestyle. Attitude is everything. With an attitude of gratitude, you will gain altitude.

> *"As a man thinketh in his heart, so is he."*
> Proverbs 23:7

> **From education comes elevation, and thus, you deserve celebration.**

My passion and discovery of celebrating others became my reward where all saw first-hand what truly can be done if everyone worked together for the common good. Seeing a project through to its completion involves a demonstration of hard work, a willingness to commit, and the fortitude to see and correct what others declined to do.

> *"Opportunities are usually disguised by hard work. So, most people don't recognize them."*
>
> Ann Landers

You will find some terms in this book are repeated throughout. We do this to better edify understanding of the material, as they relate to more than just one skill.

As you reach the end of this body of work, my hope is that you will have gained greater insight into how to implement and understand the purpose for Life Skills, why they are necessary, and how they can—and will—change your life when put into action. These skills can help you find your path to greater achievement. Let's begin by assessing **The Skill of Administration.**

Sincerely,

Mary J. Goodwin-Clinkscale, Th. D., C. Ed. D.

(a.k.a. M.J., Dr. C)

All of us do not have equal talent, but we should all have equal opportunity to develop our talents.

Oprah Winfrey

CHAPTER I:

The Skill of Administration

I AM ONLY ONE VOICE. TOGETHER WE ARE MANY.

*If you delegate tasks,
you will raise up doers.
If you delegate authority,
you will raise up leaders.*

Craig Groeschel

What is an Administrator?

An administrator is one who ties together the needs beneficial to an organization to achieve a realistic goal. It is also a person with the ability as a manager or executive to oversee the affairs of an organization. My experiences in administration began within the walls of the church and then spread abroad. As an administrator, I assisted the Pastor in helping direct the affairs of the organization and tend to the needs of the church by organizing and overseeing many events and activities.

The late Robert L. Katz, who taught in the graduate schools of business at Harvard and Stanford, published an article entitled "Skills of an Effective Administrator" in the September 1974 issue of *Harvard Business Review*.

Taking hints from his own experience, Katz suggested that becoming an excellent leader is made possible through the honing of certain levels of skill: *technical* skill, *human* skill, and *conceptual* skill. Let us take this concept a step further: leaders whose careers are at the beginning of their list of accomplishments have inborn but undeveloped God-given talents that must be developed. Regardless of one's current level of talent, they must strive continually to perfect each. As we examine each skill separately, let us realize the importance of how each of these skills are related to one another.

Any leader, even a young prodigy with innate talents from an early age, must be developed to embody the concepts of what the organization needs. Cultivating a life of change, progress, and achievement requires moving with purpose and persistence. This plan of action involves continually building bridges of collaboration and planting *seeds of hope*. Being hopeful and anticipating, these seeds will blossom into an enjoyable, peaceable life for yourself and others.

> *Leadership and learning are indispensable to each other.*
> President John Fitzgerald Kennedy

To be entrusted in a position of leadership or administration, one must accept the responsibilities that accompany the role, in order to create a lasting impact. This position involves a willingness to adopt the organization's vision, mission, and values.

Like a teacher, the administrator must understand the organizational ideals, and incorporate the unique needs of the personnel (students) and relate the requirements of the business vision (the curriculum) into the overall implementation plan.

Actually, there are many administrative qualities that relate to being an educator. The most impactful and memorable teachers tend to be the ones who have not only the technical knowledge about their subject matter but also the life experiences to share with their students. These experiences often entail both failures and successes. Remember: success does not come without learning from failure.

In addition to valuing successes and failures from our life experiences, the lifelong benefits of a *formal education* cannot be underestimated. Students must be willing to "plant" themselves into their seats to receive the necessary nourishment for increased knowledge. This concept of "teachability" lends educators "good ground" from which they may cultivate the skills they need. Still, the development of widely applicable life skills is a vital part to the education that occurs beyond classroom walls.

At first glance, the idea of administration as a life skill may be considered *unconventional,* but unless the administrator possesses these skills himself, it's nearly impossible to teach or even recognize the value life skills add to life. To perform successfully as an administrator, one must first be willing to learn, and then impart this new wisdom and knowledge to others.

As we previously stated, in his research on administration, Katz emphasized three components for optimal proficiency of skill: *people* (or *human* skill), *conceptual,* and *technical*—each of which are crucial to mastering administration as a life skill. We will give through unique examples, advice covering each one of these, and discuss how managing people can be likened to the art of cultivating a garden. A thought to keep in mind while reading this work comes from an old proverb: "You reap what you sow." II Corinthians 9:6 confirms this proverb.

> *...He which soweth sparingly shall reap also sparingly; and he which soweth bountifully shall reap also bountifully.*
>
> II Corinthians 9:6

People/Human Skill

It is usually regarded as a great compliment to have "good people skills." People, or *human* skill, is one of the most valuable skills one who manages can possess. It is the skill concerned with how to promote teamwork, handle differences of opinions or backgrounds, or how to make team members feel valued and heard. Good people skills enable you to conversate, to assimilate, and to adapt to others' personalities. Without them, an administrator would have difficulty passing on the mantle. While not impossible, it is also more challenging to be in administration if you are primarily an introvert. Administration, on the other hand, takes being ready to exit your comfort zone in order to help others.

Administrators work with individuals on multiple levels, not just ones of leadership. A good administrator encourages individuals to go above and beyond what is asked of them by their own example, while supporting their desires to do so. The proficiency at which people accomplish this essential task is what human skill embodies.

With my love of the outdoors and working in a garden, I have often compared my favorite pastime of gardening to working with people. Gardening is the cultivation of plants, from preparing the soil, to weeding, to harvesting the fruits and vegetables. This is mirrored on a grander scale by the terms, *agriculture* and *horticulture*, which are the study of the preparation and cultivation of the soil for plants to grow, and the art, science and study of living things that grow up from the ground or vine, in addition to their conservation and restoration.

As administrator of the GBT Children's Academy, it was my desire to incorporate an outdoor classroom to include a vegetable garden. The academy students ranged in ages six weeks through thirteen. We created an outdoor setting where they all could learn and observe where much of the food they consumed came from, how and where it gets produced, and why it is necessary for our continual growth, nourishment, and survival. Some of the vegetables we planted were tomatoes, cabbage, green beans, corn, broccoli, radishes onions, and different types of leafy greens, such as spinach, turnips, mustard, collards, kale, and swiss chard. The children thoroughly enjoyed participating in this activity. They enjoyed being outdoors digging in the dirt, helping to make the soil ready for spring planting.

Some of them even enjoyed picking up and playing with the earthworms, also known as fishing worms or nightcrawlers, a well-known bait used by fishermen. We were able to share how the worms contributed to the growth of the plants by helping to break down the decaying matter in the soil. They are an important and necessary food for birds. We also had visits from the bunny rabbits. As cute as they were, they were not welcome in the garden, especially since they loved to nibble on the young, thriving leafy-green plants. We had to install a rabbit fence to discourage their entrance or we would not have had a harvest to reap.

In addition to the vegetable garden we incorporated an herb garden; cultivated and maintained by the Director of the Academy, Mrs. Clute. Herb plants whether fresh or dried, are primarily used for seasoning or adding flavor to foods. She enjoyed gardening and supported the idea of an outdoor classroom for the enrichment and development of the children. Some of the herbs included thyme, sage, lemon balm, fennel, basil, and chives. Also included in that space was a strawberry patch. Not just the children, but also the adults looked forward to the reaping of the juicy red strawberries.

Mrs. Clute also incorporated an indoor Aero garden which grows and produces vegetables and herbs all year round. Aero garden lights bring sunshine indoors for fast, healthy growth using fluorescent lighting, and grows plants in water not soil. This allowed the children to observe their growth on a daily basis.

My background and experience in gardening, and my appreciation for fresh food and its health benefits, caused me to want to share and instill in these children the importance of healthy eating. On one occasion, an Omaha World Herald photojournalist Mr. Rudy Smith, visited the Academy and observed the children harvesting vegetables. He was highly impressed with the lessons being introduced to these students at such young age. As a result, he took pictures of them carrying out this activity and later published an article in the local newspaper.

How exciting! We were pleased that he wanted to share what we were implementing at the Academy with the city of Omaha. This is just one of many examples that show these interrelated skills in action, incorporating people skills, promoting teamwork, and giving the children a chance to feel valued and heard while learning.

Omaha World Herald, Midlands Section, September 2007

A ripening connection to the land

Figure 2: Four-year-old Jackson Walls, left, and Dylan Clute harvest produce they and classmates at GBT Children's Academy, 1502 N. 52nd Street, planted this spring. The youngsters planted corn, tomatoes, peppers, cucumbers, squash, onions, and pumpkins.

The love and care given for the growing and developing of a garden, *is the same love and care* that must be cultivated in the education of a **garden of people—***sowing seeds of hope*. An educator must not only have a deep-seeded desire to draw out the best in people, but also to nurture them with a genuine concern for what they need. It was often stated at my church, GBT, that leaders must have the people of God at heart, and that we are to love one another because love is of God. *Love is patient, love is kind, it does not envy, it does not boast, love is not proud, it does not dishonor others.* (I Corinthians 13: 4-5a (NIV))

> *Beloved, let us love one another: for love is of God; and everyone that loveth is born of God, and knoweth God… for God is love.*
>
> 1 John 4:7-8

There are times when plants need pruning or rearranging to grow in a more productive and visually-pleasing fashion. This redirects the nutrients to promote optimal growth. This process must be done periodically. A plant's development requires a consistent amount of sunshine and rain to be fruitful. Otherwise, the lack of care stunts growth, causes overcrowding, and can even choke out the development of some good plants, resulting in a less productive harvest.

> *For as the rain cometh down, and the snow from heaven, and returneth not thither, but watereth the earth, and maketh it bring forth and bud, that it may give seed to the sower, and bread to the eater.*
>
> Isaiah 55:10

On a similar vein, this same process applies to developing people. Sometimes the character qualities of a team member may hinder progress toward the primary goal. It is certainly an undertaking to learn the strengths of each person in your organization and where their abilities can best be applied. There are also times when change may be necessary to realign priorities or enhance your organization's growth. An administrator must exhibit firm but kind direction, especially when it involves reassigning responsibilities to maximize effectiveness.

Through the use of effective people skills, the right amount of support, cooperation, and teamwork can be cultivated. So, take courage, and know that the best can be brought out in your organization with effective implementation of these skills. Much like gardening, it requires special preparation and a little imagination to begin the development process. The art of cultivating a garden, and of developing people, when done creatively with love and care, can culminate in a form of creative beauty producing lifelong benefits *with incredible* results.

> *I have planted, Apollos watered; but God gave the increase.*
> I Corinthians 3:6

Conceptual Skill

There is a popular adage that states, "You can't see the forest for the trees." This phrase means one can become so engrossed in the details of a project (the trees), they fail to see the "big picture" (the forest). Think of having conceptual skill as having the ability to see the big picture. The word *conceptual* deals with the concepts, ideas, or principles something is based on.

Leaders must pay close attention to where the organization is heading with a project. Thus, it can be said they have a keen sense of forethought and insight into what the project should look like when completed. This embodies conceptual skill, the ability to forecast the end from the beginning in any given situation.

Moreover, having conceptual foresight involves having the ability to see the business direction as a whole, while being able to anticipate the needs of each potential problem or situation, and the possible consequences of each action. The productions implemented within Greater Beth-el Temple and GBTAA were always planned with the end in mind.

Administrators must be in tune with the overall vision to the point that it instills a sense of reverence for it in those working on the project. This is why being an effective administrator requires maintaining a vision. It is with a vision that pastors help to guide the people toward a common goal. Members can then rally around this idea and focus their efforts on promoting a unified message that is in accordance with what the leadership wishes to communicate.

The lead person of a project or group must "embody" the vision and be skilled at navigating or "steering" the overall direction of that project. Without this, mistakes can cause people to lose sight of their desired outcome and even create confusion.

Where there is no vision, the people perish.
Proverbs 29:18

Here is an example of independent and not inter-dependent leadership, an omission of conceptually-skilled oversight. There were thirteen auxiliaries and committee leaders who all worked toward common goals in our church. In one particular instance the leader and their committee were hard at work preparing for the Fourth Sunday dinner, which always involved much collaboration between that committee and members of other auxiliaries, most notably the choir.

There is a lesson to be learned here: as the Sunday service preceding the dinner progressed, the leadership in charge of special preparations for the head table were reluctant to agree to having choir participants leave to join the choir at their time. This brought up a lack of concern for the other committees involved in service. This leader felt their committee took precedence over the others because of what the status of that committee represented. The leader proved to be very dedicated to their committee, a commendable honor, but had need of being able to see the big picture of all involved.

Rather than focusing on just their auxiliary, the leader needed to understand how all auxiliaries had to function interdependently in order to work toward the unity of all under the program set forth by the administration. In order for leaders to be in harmony, they have to be focused on the one vision, or what would work best for the overall good of the church. It is important to recognize how the different auxiliaries function together and how changes in the plans of many interdependent auxiliaries affect the whole.

While participants in both these auxiliaries may still be needed to complete duties required for serving dinner, leaders should understand situations where conflicts of commitment arise. The remedy would have been to compromise by allowing the members to leave preparation to attend to their pressing matters, or using a replacement for certain individuals, or beginning their duties earlier so as not to conflict. This individual could not see the forest for the trees. They were so engrossed in the details of their own committee they failed to see the big picture.

We had since realized, as multitasking became so prevalent amongst leaders at that time, we needed to be in touch when a certain few of us became needed at the same time we were needed in another auxiliary. This committee usually began preparation for serving a Fourth Sunday dinner before morning service. Whenever this happens, one ought to consult with other leaders to make it possible for them to join forces and be on one accord. It was time to come together as an inter-dependent whole.

An *independent* person will probably not progress very far on a team, due to the fact they might not allow other individuals into their space or to govern them. A *dependent* person is even less destined to go very far, as they are limited in their creativity and in their ability to innovate themselves. An *inter-dependent* person—having grounded themselves in their own success through the success of others—will more likely progress further personally and professionally as a member of a supportive team. They rely on mutual assistance from others, yet, are genuine enough to make it happen for themselves while working in conjunction with others.

People and plants both grow to *better* adapt to their environment. The decisions leaders make are impacted by their environment, and the same is what happens to plants raised in a garden. Many blossoming plants react to the change in season, from sprouting seeds to flowering and displaying their beauty. Certain plants are intentionally planted or pruned and replanted next to a trellis, pole or fence so they may later grow and attach to it. This is an example of how plants take it upon themselves to adhere to the *concept* of *better* growth, once the *concept* of where to grow is established.

When people are planted into certain positions, they tend to apply their strengths to their job descriptions. You can tell people are in the place they are supposed to be, when they begin to show signs of mature growth, as they adapt to their new environment, through showing creativity. The tasks given to them by leaders should be carefully assessed beforehand—do they give the participant a way to be creative? Note that both plants and people have ingrained in them the *concept* of how to grow *better*, and it takes both the planter and the plant working together to produce the best intended outcome.

Technical Skill

As administrators, we should make it a priority to maintain our proficiency in, and understanding of, the techniques and methods used to enhance job performance. Being proficient in these work processes is referred to as *technical skill*. An administrator must reach out and include others to complete demanding tasks. This deletes nothing from your role as an administrator. In fact, it shows maturity on your part while developing new technical skills in others. This will not happen overnight, but instead requires time and perseverance. Time and change happen to us all, and time brings about change. As opportunities arise and individuals make themselves available, these administrative skills will blossom and lead to *greater* experiences. Such was the case with my administrative experience: each milestone led to *greater* advantages for me and my teams.

Any job performed after being taught how to incorporate or utilize all its components involves technical skill, which is sometimes referred to as on the job training. Here is an example of development of technical skill in action:

Though I was already functioning as church administrator, I was given the charge to develop the church choir as part of my administrative duties. I interacted primarily with the lead director, although I interacted with many other appointed directors across the board. These included various directors, some of whom had never directed a choir, vocalists who had never sung in a choir, and even musicians who had never played with a choir.

Every individual who expressed a desire to participate came together, each one bringing their undeveloped technical skills at the beginning. On every occasion, we prayed together, encouraging one another, and helping to instill confidence. Likely unaware to some, while we practiced together, we were supporting each other to believe that through faith, all things are possible. As the development of our techniques progressed, each instrument accompanying the voices in their respective positions, God blessed each choir participant and musician to eventually perform in a manner where the untrained eye might suspect they all attended and were taught by a professional choir director or attended a professional conservatory.

Beautiful music poured out of this amazing choir which can only be described as a wonder to behold. Voices and instruments blended together in perfect harmony, producing a choir that received rave reviews. We built on each one of our technical skills and brought it all together while incorporating all seven life skills mentioned here. I, along with the participants, learned so much about the development of, and the techniques of leading songs, intonation, and harmonizing. Truly, it can be said God blessed our combined efforts, as we lifted our voices in total praise.

It can also be said He developed our inborn abilities and talents with His amazing grace and undying love. Indeed, my God is a mighty God. His wondrous works He will unfold through faith if we only believe.

If you desire something you've never had, you must do something you've never done.

– Thomas Jefferson

Assuming a Leadership Role

In my first major position as pastor's aide auxiliary chairlady, my job was to organize and increase productivity in an auxiliary which at that time consisted of only a few members but had quickly increased to 85. With the steady growth of the organization, I needed to devise an effective plan of leadership and delegate to utilize each member's skillset.

As time passed, the job became more challenging as the church began to grow in numbers. Many individuals made themselves available to help. Two, in particular, proved to be dedicated in offering their time and talents, and eventually became my Program Assistants (PA's). Isn't it amazing how God works? He never ceases to amaze me by always having a "ram in the bush." In other words, "God will give you what you need, when you need it."

My *desire* was to prove faithful and bring to fruition what I felt would define the position to which I had been appointed. Functioning within church auxiliaries in my beginnings helped me tremendously in learning how each group functioned. It also helped me understand what potential solutions needed to be explored, in order to improve each auxiliary's effectiveness.

After being appointed to the position of church administrator, one of my responsibilities included quality assurance. I began to oversee reviewing and approving payments and reimbursements, while minimizing frivolous expenses. One of my highest priorities was to ensure funds were consistently coming into the church, and not being spent needlessly.

Being in administration requires becoming skilled at juggling tasks, being a team player, and prioritizing responsibilities – all while maintaining a state of order. As I progressed, opportunities and duties presented themselves along the way, based on a variety of different types of tasks and structural needs that arose.

Finally, being and remaining effective at leadership involves incorporating what is learned into one's own standard practices. Leading by example simply means: "Practicing what you preach." Action speaks louder than words. When people see the act, they can learn to mimic what they see. While advice is necessary, the living example that you can give as a leader is invaluable.

As an Administrator, whenever I asked for the congregation to give, whether in terms of giving monetarily, giving service, attending meetings, or supporting the youth in their endeavors, I always made myself the first to respond to the cause. It is unprofessional to be in a position of authority when you are not supportive of what you expect others to do. *Be that example*, and the people will follow. *Take my hand*, walk *with* me, and we will *grow* up *together*.

Embodying the Vision as an Administrator

Equipped with these skills (human, technical, and conceptual), administrators will be most effective in their roles when they genuinely understand the mind of their leader. In so doing, they will embody their organization's vision and mission.

These concepts and principles apply in many situations, not just in churches but also other types of businesses. The process of developing a business includes both learning the goals and mission from your leader's perspective and understanding the main conviction or vision. The vision is important because it lays out on paper the direction in which the organization is going.

Contrary to some beliefs, church **is** a business. Within the walls of many churches, the pastor is the C.E.O. chief operating officer. The Auxiliary leaders are the support systems that work to operate in a manner consistent with the vision of the church. One gets to know the pastor through his teachings and messages preached; or even through meetings outside of services or participation in church-sponsored events. Some examples along my life's path of getting to know my pastor include lessons learned from messages he preached:

- **"Living Beyond Human Feelings"**: This message reflected on the idea of receiving instructions with a positive attitude. To strive for excellence, one must put aside personal feelings to accept instruction and correction.
- **"No Respecter of Persons"**: This message detailed how the pastor's life of sacrifice was manifested before the congregation. His supreme purpose was to lift up God's people, to draw and to keep them with "cords of love." This goal included developing individuals to a greater potential.
  Likewise, my intention as an administrator was to give instruction through encouragement and correction, while developing both church and Academy members to a greater potential. This mission was made possible in part through presenting visual programs in an unconventional way, endorsing the teachings received.
- **"Passing on the Mantle"**: When God took of the spirit of Moses and put it on seventy chosen elders of Israel (Numbers 11:17), it was an example of God making the divine choice himself of setting up new leaders to assist Moses in helping to rule over the people. This scripture explains the model of how a leader ought to allow others to implement his mind, his leadership, and what he intends, using the power of their many thoughts and many hands.

> *I am not able to bear all this people alone, because it is too heavy for me.... And I will come down and talk with thee there: and I will take of the spirit which is upon thee, and will put it upon them; and they shall bear the burden of the people with thee, that thou bear it not thyself alone.*
>
> Numbers 11: 14, 17

At the start of my operating as a leader, the Pastor himself would often attend scheduled meetings. This helped us tremendously with getting to know our leader, as the questions members asked would lead to a deeper interaction between members and the Pastor. The Pastor would give his viewpoints on church policies and clarify our directions as the meeting progressed.

His participation, and even just his attendance in church sponsored events, became of great value in learning what he enjoyed, his demeanor and his disposition.

> *Wisdom is the principal thing; therefore, get wisdom: and with all thy getting get understanding.*
>
> Proverbs 4:7

Implementing Your Leader's Mind

Implementing the mind of your leader merely means compliance to authority and applying rules and regulations that have been established.

> *Obey them that have the rule over you, and submit yourselves: for they watch for your souls.*
>
> Hebrews 13:17

This is a broad and controversial subject. Some would dispute that every one of us is being governed by someone or something. We are not an island. The notion that you are your own person and subject to no one is debatable.

From the time you arrive in this world you are subject to a leader. When you were born, the doctor guided you from your mother's womb into the hands of an awaiting nurse, who coaxed you into taking your first breath. From the nurse you were guided into your mother's arms, where your first lessons in life truly began – Lesson #1: Love and affection.

From that moment on, both mother and father continue to nourish and supply you with the necessary nutrients, affection, and care for your survival, until reaching maturity. Then you come under teachers (tutors), governors (authorities), and the laws of the land, under which we all must follow.

Now... back to church.

Imagine the chaos that would ensue if each member of a congregation, business, or school decided they had no need to follow rules or laws! Isn't that the real reason why we attend church services, to gain knowledge and understanding of the world in which we live, according to the word of God? Isn't that why we attend school, to obtain an education and become productive citizens? Isn't that the same reason we desire gainful employment and advancement in our careers, to be productive citizens? I believe the answer to these questions would unquestionably be *yes.*

Servant-Based Leadership

These factors make your leadership one that serves others:

1. A servant-based leadership involves sincerity and genuine concern for others.
2. A servant-based leadership involves being selfless, and encouraging teamwork
3. A servant-based leadership involves being wholly supportive of your organization's needs.

4. A servant-based leadership helps demonstrate for members what is necessary, without always needing to tell them *how* to do it.
5. A servant-based leadership incorporates meetings that point people in the right direction by providing examples that help energize members.
6. A servant-based leadership allows for time to take suggestions from members to gain diverse input.
7. A servant-based leadership recalls historical events by holding celebrations to commemorate successful achievements.

How does an Aide/Director/Assistant help carry out these convictions? By following the leader. Since the leader cannot do it all, the leader delegates tasks to the followers. If you're ever wondering how to accomplish an overwhelming amount of work, just think back to following the leader. We have more on principles of leadership to come in Chapter III.

It's in giving that we receive, and in serving that we find ourselves.
—Brendon Burchard

Enhancing Teaching Methods

Involving team members in the planning process is a method that was used at GBT to help increase learning. To be effective, administrators must teach the process others need to follow in a way that is easily understood. As leaders, we must uphold a standard that everyone is expected to follow. An individual's style of learning will affect how easy it is for them to learn (See Learning Styles in Chapter IV). If material is meaningful to a person, he is more apt to pick up the concept quickly. Well-placed mnemonics (memory aids) can help others grasp the main idea, so they walk away remembering it at the end of the meeting.

As a leader, don't forget to keep in mind the progress your team has made toward success. Take the initiative to make others aware of how far they have come. Success is something every member of a team ought to be proud of.

Awareness of progress can be a motivator. As leaders, we must realize that success does not come without making mistakes. We should learn from our mistakes and failures, as the pain behind failure helps us improve our techniques, and they make us into the well-rounded individuals we ought to be.

Take note of both successes, and of methods that have worked best, as you progress. Help your team recall outstanding instances of their performance that could have been done **better**, while commending a job well done with due praise.

Set Clear Expectations

And the Lord answered me: "Write the vision; make it plain on tablets, so he may run who reads it.
Habakkuk 2:2

The most important role of a leader is to set a clear direction, be transparent about how to get there and to stay the course.
Irene Rosenfeld

For an organization to be successful, the vision must be clearly defined so that all members may understand. Administrators help the members discover areas within the church where help is needed, particularly regarding individual roles, goals, and expectations. Answering the questions below will help bring clarity to define the organization's membership needs and sense of belonging.

- What are the goals of the church (as outlined by the leader or pastor)?
- What are the commitments to the church/community?
- Who is needed to fulfill these goals?
- What goals are set for these individuals?
- What role does each participating individual play?

By evaluating these, your leadership and the method of implementing the mind of your leader will foster success. Specific roles are needed within the church community. These roles are often long-term commitments to serve. Each role is acknowledged by title and responsibility. Remember, also:

1. First and foremost, understand the function and responsibility of these roles.
2. Expect all to perform as leaders within their roles.
3. Understand the reporting structure for each role.
4. Keep it simple.

The church is the vessel for the facilitation of all things. In other words, the church building is the instrument given to deliver on the needs of its local congregation and community. Following are some helpful tips to keep in mind at the time you begin planning the use of church areas for functions:

1. Have a profound pride in the presentation of EVERYTHING within the church and hold it to its utmost standards.
2. Have a detail-oriented person involved in all planning.
3. Gather feedback from the individuals that are using planned event areas to see if the current setup in each room facilitates the event being held there.
4. Assess the needs of each specific area, i.e. kitchen, hall, dining room, and sanctuary etc.…
5. Evaluate the organization of artifacts or props within these areas.

6. Arrange parts of a room to serve specific functions.
7. Have all parts work together to complete an overall theme.

Working as an administrator, you will certainly encounter stress. The responsibility of juggling these countless tasks naturally brings about a sense of urgency to get the job done. The amount of work you put forth, in terms of energy and in terms of time, may contribute to a rise in stress to get it all done. You must gauge carefully how much energy you expend in a day, or you will surely overtax yourself.

Managing Administrative Stress

Although some stress is normal, much stress can cause problems with both your health and in dealing with others. The body's natural responses to stress change how you feel and how you act. However, there are specific signs that need to be heeded, as they may indicate health problems. If you experience multiple signs out of the following listed, consider changing how you deal with the stressors you may be experiencing.

- Muscle tension, stiffness
- Stiff neck and shoulder pain
- Physical and mental pressure
- Increased heart rate, palpitations
- Headaches / migraines
- Restlessness, or inability to sleep
- Overeating leading to weight gain
- Lack of appetite, leading to malnourishment
- Irritable, easily annoyed
- Feeling anxious or depressed

Healthy and Unhealthy Stress

As mentioned earlier, even though I have retired from the pressure and stress of working in an administrative position, I've since taken on the job of writing this book, and it has had its stressors as well.

Although some stress can be healthy, as it keeps the mind alert and active, stress in excess can become unhealthy, causing irritability and feeling discouraged.

Stress can also come from how we deal with other individuals. There are times situations may arise, and times where they can be difficult to clear up. Depending on the nature or severity, some problems are best left alone. In time, the issue will resolve or take care of itself.

Stress cannot be completely eliminated; it is something we must learn to endure. On the other hand, it is wise to keep a balance between resolving stressful situations and relaxing; your health is a vital factor and should not be taken for granted as – this is *your* life. Make your plan and stick to your plan, devoting your time and energy to tackling what's most important.

Finally, the benefits of fostering relationships with positive people can lower your stress level. At all times, try to operate in a supportive environment. If you find you are continually living in a stressful environment, begin to evaluate your associations. Remember that you can be influenced by positive and negative attitudes.

Organizing Your Auxiliary: Action Items

As church administrator, one of my primary roles was to oversee auxiliary and committee leaders. This responsibility included educating leaders to develop a shared vision and purpose for their team.

Here are some foundations you as an administrator should develop at the start, to help you organize your team.

1. **Mission Statement:** To help understand the responsibility of your auxiliary, you should develop a mission statement. Take the initiative to see that all actions of your team follow the mission statement. Also, develop a vision to go with your mission, to lay out a clear path dictating where you plan for your auxiliary to go.
2. **Organizational Structure:** Spend some time spelling out the important key roles the organization needs to function, taking special care to explain what they mean. All members will then be clear on what responsibilities those who hold the office ought to be held accountable for. To start this process, determine the strengths and weaknesses of team members. The opinions of the team members should be considered at this point. It gives them a chance to express their own desires for the positions or the teams in which they would like to function.

    Next, quickly determine officers related to carrying out auxiliary responsibilities for each position. Again, make it clear. The last thing to be done when organizing auxiliary structure is to assign titles that describe their responsibilities. The structured plan of who is doing what can also be used to define the titles themselves. The leader should try to describe what a person does in a simple, yet descriptive-enough way, so that others know who to go to for help when they need it.
3. **Business Plan:** Now that people have roles and responsibilities, leaders under the main administration can easily start laying out for themselves a set of goals for their groups, which will soon add up to be the set of goals the whole auxiliary is aiming to achieve. Each of these leaders should submit their worked-out plan of action to you for approval. Perhaps they were tasked

with coming up with different plans for different goals. Perhaps they were tasked with plans all achieving the same goal. Regardless, you as the administrator should take all into consideration to address each later in an *overall plan of action*. This will consist of the most concrete description of your thoughts on how to achieve *your own administrative* goals for the auxiliary.

Short and Long-Term Goals

Goals that you have are typically categorized into two groups, short- and long-term, based on how much time you have for each task. Preparing for short and long-term goals involves motivating leaders to bring their teams to a higher level. The following are some objectives to support this effort:

- Encourage your team to communicate the goals and objectives of your vision.
- Encourage people to follow others who are promoting your goals.
- Encourage individuals to participate in activities that bring out their strengths.
- Encourage teamwork attributes and enforce rules and regulations continually.
- Encourage, develop and always maintain the right attitude at all times, especially during meetings.
- Encourage and assist auxiliary members in understanding how to perform at home and abroad.

In addition, you must consider the maximum amount of time you can expend. An example of a short-term goal might be, "The academy needs to complete the writing of our next script in three weeks." Another example is "the completion of this book is destined to happen in the next few months." In contrast, an example of a long-term goal is: I plan to complete a second book in the span of my lifetime. Different amounts of time will be allotted for these two types of projects as well. You have to allot the appropriate amount of time toward achieving set goals. Regardless of how challenging this is, don't give up and don't give in; it will be well worth your effort in the end.

Qualities of an Effective Leader

To be an effective administrator or leader, one must...

- Be willing to follow while leading
- Commit to time beyond the norm
- Share ideas, interests and dreams
- Accept feedback
- Be an assertive advocate
- Energize others to reach their full potential
- Prepare for candid, open and honest discussion
- Use appropriate humor to "lighten the load"
- Be a motivator, not an authoritarian
- Identify skills needed for leaders
- Define specific roles within an organization
- Be willing to invest your time, talents and resources

Inspired Teaching

It is unquestionable that being an inspiration to your students involves knowing how to educate and how ideas are best conveyed through words. What makes the difference is knowing how to bring out the best in your students. These tips speak to the notion of being an empowering, inspirational teacher.

1. Inspired teaching stems from your passion to empower and is contagious. Some learn best by observing examples you bring to the table. What others see you do, they are inclined to follow.

2. Your method of teaching can help bring out the aptitudes your students have and show how their talents matter in the classroom. Inspired teaching is about developing minds, skills and talents, and about showing that you care.
3. Staying up to date on current facts is a must for a teacher to be effective and relatable. Staying relevant and inspired by your environment can be what keeps your teaching on the same page with what is taught in other curriculums.
4. When people see you motivated and animated, it makes them more responsive and brings about a more engaging dialogue between you and your students.
A teacher who is a good listener indicates someone mature and educated enough on a topic to discuss it.
5. The way material is taught should change from time to time. Inspired teaching is about being brave enough to embrace change.

Improving Your Administrative Skills

As an administrator, you may find it rewarding to bring others into the process of developing new leaders.

An effective leader is not an autocrat, which means he does not work alone. He values input from his learners and is more of a guide than a dictator.

The leader holds a different responsibility than other members of the group: a leader must have the mind of leaders above them. Meanwhile they remain accountable for what they implement, reporting to their own leaders with feedback on what they've accomplished.

It bears repeating:

- A good leader delegates and distributes responsibility and builds on the strengths of others.
- A good leader has the responsibility to judge the group on their accomplishments and share their evaluations with the group on how well they're doing.
- A good leader maintains self-control while managing those they lead. They take on the responsibility to create situations in which people can willingly give their best.

Creating a situation that promotes such an environment takes being organized. This takes us into **The Skill of Organization**: *the key to all successful organizations.*

Quotes on Administration

Some of the best lessons we ever learn are learned from past mistakes. The error of the past is the wisdom and success of the future.

Dale Turner

Success is to be measured not so much by the position one has reached, but more so by the obstacles which we overcome while trying to succeed.

Booker T. Washington

Scriptures on Administration

And there are differences of administration, but the same Lord.

I Corinthians 12:5

For the administration of this service not only supplieth the want of the saints, but is abundant also by many thanksgivings unto God.

II Corinthians 9:12

CHAPTER II:

The Skill of Organization

To all who wish to transform their lives from a chaotic state, to a life that is organized, logical, balanced and functional, my advice is that you be not conformed [to this chaotic state] but be ye transformed by the renewing of your mind.

And be not conformed to this world: but be ye transformed by the renewing of your mind, that ye may prove what is that good, and acceptable, and perfect, will of God.

Romans 12:1,2

What is organization?

Organization is a way of life. It involves aligning processes into an optimal working order that incorporates individuals who are united for a common goal. When you assemble a group of individuals who work as a cohesive unit to achieve a specific goal or purpose, you have the foundation of a system with almost limitless potential.

Organization is the act of putting things in order. It is also known by the words *planning, arrangement,* or *coordination.* The act of organizing involves arranging things into a structured whole.

An organization is also a group of persons united for some purpose. Churches are one type of organization. An organizer brings ideas into being or action or brings parts together.

Perceptions on Implementing Organization

Every establishment has its own values and organizational structure. Likewise, each church is unique in how it functions. A church will have its own administration, set of standards, terminology, and definition of how it is governed.

Quite often, start-up churches, as well as established ones, struggle with how to operate in a synergistic manner. Come with me, as I take you down a path that has worked for many who have joined the teams of hard-workers assembled within the walls of the sanctuary.

My experience in organization was catapulted to another level when I began volunteering my services in a variety of areas throughout the church. When I was appointed to various positions, I accepted each one with pleasure and zeal, not knowing completely what the position entailed. There were no clear directions or instructions given for what was required. It was almost as if I was expected to come with a set of directives that would automatically fulfill every request.

Each experience was a powerful lesson. With much deliberation, and through trial and error, I began to formulate ideas that I believed would **better** define the responsibilities of these jobs, so they worked for the good of the church.

As with any job, you will increase in learning as you perform the responsibilities that the job entails, and you should always be willing to expand your horizon. You may learn you are meant for a 'higher calling' (or elevation) because of your performance, commitment and dedication to the job. In many cases, you are already performing the duties required of your next position before it is awarded to you.

As I began this journey, little did I realize the satisfaction and education I would receive, would all stem from a need for **better**. This need included the indoctrination into the Word of God, which I soon discovered to be the main ingredient for a **better** life.

Building upon the skill of organization came through implementing the mind of my leader, who was my pastor. This concept of implementing the mind of your leader can be applied not only in church, but in the workplace, and literally every facet of life.

The programs and events produced at GBT involved multiple teaching methods, including visual demonstrations. These unconventional techniques were an effective way to educate and engage the members. Getting to know the governing of your own congregation will help determine the most impactful and accepted way to implement organization within your church or group.

While approaching my transition to retirement a few years ago, I began receiving requests to visit other churches as a consultant and share **better** practices for organization.

I am humbled by the people's belief in my abilities, and in gratitude of the life skills God has granted me, I am compelled to share my experiences with you.

Why organize?

Organization is the key to everything you attempt in your lifetime. It saves time, effort and energy, and gives you a sense of control. Order creates serenity, confidence and peace of mind. When brought to fruition, it becomes synergy, which means uniting the work of a few to result in an effect seemingly put on by many. This process can be compared to [God's] people operating together as a well-oiled machine in the body of Christ.

> *In Africa, we have a saying, 'If you want to go fast, go alone. If you want to go far, go together.' ...Consider us... Ponder what it would be like if we went together. Not alone and fast but together and far.*
>
> Robin Jones Gunn

Organization in the Home

A wise saying often repeated states, "Charity (love) begins at home and spreads abroad." While this is not stated verbatim in the Bible, the concept is described:

> *"But if any widow have children or nephews, let them learn first to shew piety [devoutness] at home, and to requite their parents: for that is good and acceptable before God."*
>
> 1 Timothy 5:4

Organization relieves pressure and can result in a more peaceable life, which should begin at home. Children should be taught and expected to execute organizational skills and have a place for all things.

The life lessons in development absent during the upbringing of children leave them devoid (lacking) of purpose and challenged to deal with their issues on their own, thus questioning how to handle them in a more mature way. Often, children are left alone to fend for themselves, many times in a desperate attempt to resolve their own disorders. On the other hand, teaching children organizational *skills* in the home can produce lifelong contentment. Introducing concepts like this early on simplifies a child's thought process and provides means to achieve their goals faster.

Having an organized space will allow you to reap numerous (and obvious) benefits. Have a designated place for everything and return to its proper place everything you take out, so you won't waste time trying to find it. This will allow you time to focus on other areas of concern.

Anyone who can demonstrate organizational *skills* is a person who possesses a keen sense of self, and therefore recognizes what's important to the overall advancement of any project. This *improvement skill* evolves into a practice that will last a lifetime.

An Organization's Core Values

Acknowledging your beliefs in your organization's mission, core values and vision, helps what you've started feel genuine to people, and helps employees function more naturally. Following are some ways to incorporate values into your mission.

When you develop core values, remember that people are expected to follow them, so don't leave out key factors or compromise what you believe to be right.

1. Aim high but publish realistic expectations. Realize that people are human and have limitations on their time and resources.
2. Interweave words into your written set of values which encourage employees/students to influence and persuade others to adopt them into their lifestyle.
3. Seek ways to increase how effective the organization can be by evaluating what you are doing against what you want to be doing.

4. Incorporate ways to make work more exciting and thought- provoking on a continual basis.

Leaders should have an innate desire to maintain excellence; they should be intent on promoting their organization's values as they inspire others to succeed.

Planning and Why Plan

We have discussed what organization is, why we organize, how it is used in the home, and how to develop core values in your organization. It has been said, and bears repeating, 'if you fail to plan, you plan to fail.' *Planning* ensures that a method is worked out beforehand to accomplish an objective. *Planning* is just another form of organization involving a variety of steps: preparation, arrangement, scheduling, and designing. The importance of *planning* begins with you. Setting up a process for *planning* results in *better* performance and promotes success by promoting teamwork.

You should begin *planning* with the outcome in mind. As stated earlier, our Creator began His creation with a plan. He did His work in such a timely manner, accomplishing His creation of the world in six days. After seeing that "It was good" on the seventh day, He rested from his work.

Visualizing and documenting a path for your team involves setting goals that include every member, goals that may be challenging, but are yet attainable. Creating a vision with steps that are clearly outlined helps others embrace the plan for success and keeps individuals from becoming too content with the status quo.

This next section describes some examples of *planning* as it relates to organizing special programs and events that occurred in the church.

Forming a Planning Committee

Many programs in the church were planned throughout the years of my tenure as Chairlady. The Planning Committee, which consisted of both auxiliary leaders and lay members, was established as an effective method to prepare for these productions. The committee members who participated varied with each occasion, and we always welcomed new participants. This activity proved to be an excellent opportunity for the church to become more actively involved. It was both educational and enlightening, and our administration encouraged church involvement, togetherness and teamwork.

While some programs delivered a more serious message, like the Pastoral Anniversary, others incorporated amusing elements, most notably birthday parties. Entertainment and humor were always a welcomed addition to our presentations. It reflected the personalities of our leaders and helped the congregation identify with the message being illustrated.

The Planning Committee developed an effective process for preparing programs, which include the following steps:

1. Brainstorm for ideas and possible themes
2. Decide key scripture and general program format
3. Break into sub-committees
4. Write script, re-write script, edit, and revise
5. Identify characters and actors
6. Rehearse, rehearse, rehearse (fine-tune)
7. Final presentation

Brainstorming Sessions

For each occasion, the first order of business was to select a theme. During these brainstorming sessions, we would consider the overall purpose of the program, be it an anniversary, birthday, or holiday. Later, we would try to demonstrate the mind of the leaders in a way the congregation/audience would understand. The message can be clearly portrayed when it relates to topics recently taught or discussed.

Once the committee has generated a list of possible themes, one would be selected with the following considerations in mind:

1. capture the mind of the leaders and the audience
2. easily lend itself to the development of a program
3. relates to current news and events
4. ease of ability to present visually

A selection of our programs and themes:

- **I Believe I Can Fly** (Pastoral/Church Anniversary) (Topic chosen to encourage and uplift the church. Also, used later with GBT Academy of the Arts to honor the World War II veterans, the Tuskegee Airmen.)
- **Guilty / Not Guilty of Showing Appreciation** (Pastoral/Church Anniversary) (incorporated characters from O.J. Simpson trial combined with the award-winning "Forrest Gump" movie, with Forrest being guilty of showing appreciation.)
- **Branson Brings Precious Moments** (Holiday Dinner) (Selected to share trip experience to Branson, Missouri, and Precious Moments headquarters, located in Carthage, Missouri, with members who were unable to attend.)
- **Y2K: Just Another Day** (Pastoral/Church Anniversary) (tied to current events related to the year 2000, a.k.a. the Millennium)
- **9-11 Wake Up Call: Choose Life** (Pastoral/Church Anniversary) (following the bombing of 9/11, 2001)

- **An Enchanted Evening** (50th Wedding Anniversary) (An unforgettable celebration of the love between two individuals that stood the test of time.)
- **Following Stars in Search of an Extraordinary King** (Holiday Dinner) (Incorporated portrayals of Michael Jackson, Dr. Martin Luther King Jr., B.B. King and Elvis Presley the King on the path to locate the true King.) In this case the Extraordinary King was the Pastor.
- **A Living History:** The Struggle for Equality (Black History Program)

Determine key scripture and general program format

After choosing the program theme, we selected scriptures the Pastor emphasized in prior messages to accompany the theme. From that list, one main scripture was chosen as the focus.

Current news and events in the community and the nation were considered as an innovative way to engage and educate the intended audience. Making the message relatable enhances the probability of a better, overall understanding.

A good program must have a good vehicle, or method of presentation, and should communicate the theme in an entertaining fashion. Much thought went into how to present our ideas, and the format differed depending on whether we were in the sanctuary or somewhere else such as another church, a hotel, a banquet hall or convention center. The layout and size of the venue determined what items and activities could be employed.

Break into sub-committees

Once a theme and format were confirmed, we formed groups and spent time doing research for each part of the program. If we were referencing a movie or a book, it had to be reviewed to select the portions that pertained to our theme. Songs were selected, and in nearly all cases, were rearranged to identify with the theme, thereby creating a unique rendition.

Supporting scriptures were interweaved into the program, but always in harmony with the overall purpose.

Write and rewrite script, edit, and revise

The next step is writing the script. Those who had the ability and were willing to write were given these assignments and worked with those who wished to have their talents developed. A timeline would be established for the completion of the first draft. The group then met to review it. We would edit the script, refine the message, and identify where scriptures and songs could be inserted. This process requires determination, patience, scrutiny and revision.

Identify characters and actors

Factors considered in selecting potential cast members are:

- Age-appropriateness for the roles
- A demeanor similar to the character of the part
- Willingness to work
- Availability for practice
- Attitude toward constructive criticism
- Capability to perform

The ultimate selection of actors is based on these qualities, their performance and overall attitude.

No individual who participated in these activities received monetary compensation. Through working together, becoming team players, and communicating a common message in an uncommon way, they were compensated by not only receiving increased wisdom, knowledge and understanding in the subject matter, but also insights on life itself.

Rehearse, rehearse, rehearse (fine-tune)

Throughout the years, we created programs that would appeal to our Pastor and his wife. We were not hearers only, but also doers, "performers", of the spoken Word of God (James 1:22). My aim was to create programs they would enjoy by inserting points of interest relating to their lives. To please others, you must give them what they want and enjoy, not what you want and enjoy.

In giving of yourself, you may reap not only added benefits of personal enjoyment but also educational benefits. In the end you will be truly blessed by all the time you give of yourself for the benefit of others.

Being willing to give the time required for numerous rehearsals was an integral part to each program's success. Striving for perfection was the goal, and preparation was the process. The theme was fine-tuned through the rehearsals, and a key component to this step was in the planning process. Parts were rehearsed in sections and then brought together. A series of rehearsals were scheduled to bring together all components and adjust where necessary.

Dress rehearsal was imperative. When performing at a hotel, we rehearsed on location, and if that was not possible, we would improvise with a made-to-scale stage at the church. Placement of the performers and the delivery of their lines must all be fine-tuned. Other individuals were appointed over the music, costumes, programming, and stage design.

The way a message is presented determines how it is received, so we always tried to present programs in a way the audience could relate. Know your audience and tailor your communication accordingly.

The Final Presentation

The culmination of this entire process is the final presentation. Again, individuals were placed in positions of responsibility at designated location to ensure the proper execution of the program. If we were successful in the delivery of the theme, whether by use of humor, drama, music, song or dance, a message was being portrayed and the audience would leave with greater insight to the message being communicated.

Coordinating Group Travel

Another area requiring organization was making travel arrangements for large groups. Many trips were coordinated over the years. The trips made to Branson, Missouri, to single out one destination, proved to be memorable and extremely enlightening. Representing a diverse group of individuals from various backgrounds, I was challenged to motivate the group by sharing reasons why a trip to Branson would be enjoyable, informative and educational. Located in the heart of the Ozarks, Branson offers not only country and western performances but other genres of music and good family entertainment. It has been said that Branson is "Little Las Vegas without the gambling." This is perhaps due to all the beautiful theaters and the inviting attractions tourists are exposed to when they travel there.

The process of planning a multi-day bus tour requires months of preparation in advance, depending on the availability of shows and the number of individuals participating in the excursion. Organizing between 47-54 reservations for everyone on the bus involved careful, consistent communication with the travel agency as well as arrangements for a chartered bus.

Explicit instructions and attention to detail were necessary to ensure an enjoyable trip for all.

Hotel arrangements must be carefully planned, and many factors taken into consideration, including the type and number of rooms needed, number of individuals per room, and preferred floor level. Whether your requests are granted by the hotel is contingent upon availability for the time requested. Keeping in contact with the travel agency is imperative, however. It's important to check periodically to ensure your party is still in the registration system before you arrive, as human errors are made daily. Fortunately, we never incurred any such incident.

Another factor that requires your undivided attention is the collection and disbursement of monies, which can be very taxing and time-consuming. The number of people attending determines when the deposit for each show must be remitted. Some shows require deposits six months in advance, while others require only two or three.

If these requirements are executed, you and your party should enjoy a much-anticipated excursion.

Pre-Trip Meeting

To organize a trip for a large group, we held a meeting with all participants planning to travel. Each item of concern is addressed—in particular, what is to be expected when traveling on a tour bus with a group of so many passengers. The tour bus would typically arrive one-and-a-half hours prior to the scheduled departure to allow individuals time to load their belongings and find their assigned seating. There was also reserved seating for persons with special needs.

These expectations, which will be described in detail, include:

- Organized packing
- Personal hygiene
- One's diet
- Restroom breaks
- Snacks
- Itinerary

These prior considerations make for a more enjoyable trip. To reiterate, if you fail to plan, you plan to fail.

Organized Packing

It is important to create a packing list and check off each item as it is packed. Following is a photograph of a sample packing arrangement and related items. This arrangement was completed by my 13-year-old granddaughter who grew up in the GBT Academy of the Arts alongside her parents who were active Academy participants and excellent organizers. She was preparing for a week-long summer youth leadership program held at a prestigious, Midwestern state university.

Making a list virtually eliminates forgetting important items needed for travel. My granddaughter called her organized packing list an "inverted pyramid of clothes". She literally laid out her items on the bedroom floor, starting with the largest item of each group, and ending with the smallest of clothing, laying them into a pyramid to ensure she had a visual of every item needed for her trip. She then checked off each item after collecting it for packing. As an alternative, your bed may be used for arranging items.

Her process for creating this list is as follows:

1. Roll clothes tightly, (rather than folding them) to create added space in your luggage.
2. Group like items together.
3. Pack slippers and shower shoes to protect your feet from areas that may not be properly disinfected.
4. Include bathing items like a loofa or wash cloth, shampoo, conditioner, body wash or soap, and required personal items.
5. Wrap shoes in plastic bags to protect them from potentially soiling other items of clothing when packed in the same baggage.
6. Use a smaller tote for certain items to make them easily accessible (such as a carry-on bag used when flying), which might include a light jacket or sweater, umbrella, sunglasses, phone, reading materials, and purse or wallet, etc.
7. In her case, a designated bag for snacks in lodging area was required.
8. Pack outfits according to the type of weather, occasion or activity for which you are traveling, such as jeans, shorts, sweatshirts, pajamas, and outfits for planned outdoor activities. Plan for the unexpected.
9. Take a bag for dirty items to prevent mixing clean and soiled laundry.
10. Bring any necessary medications needed during your travel.

Although this is a young teenager preparing for travel, the process is applicable to any age.

Whenever the GBT Academy group traveled by plane, we recommended participants save on baggage fees by sharing one piece of luggage with their roommate – when trips were brief. This concept was accomplished by separating each person's belongings with plastic dry-cleaner bags. The notion was accepted, and it proved to be successful as each learned a valuable lesson to incorporate into their future travels.

Personal Hygiene

Be mindful of your personal hygiene. Be sure to shower prior to boarding the bus, or whatever mode of transportation is used. Use deodorant, and wear freshly laundered clothes, clean socks and shoes. Avoid excessive use of perfumes as some persons may have allergies or sensitivity to strong scents, especially those who may be sitting next to or behind you.

Just imagine sitting adjacent to an individual who worked all day and didn't take these precautionary measures. You then would have quite the adventure for the next umpteen hours of travel! We certainly do not want to offend our sisters and brothers (fellow passengers).

Diet

Be cautious of food intake the day of planned travel and while traveling. Avoid those items which may not agree with your digestive system. This cautionary measure also includes avoiding drinking an excessive amount of liquids. The importance of monitoring your consumption of food cannot be over-emphasized. We've all experienced upset stomachs —the untimeliness of this unfortunate situation is certainly undesirable while in transit.

Snacks

When traveling by b us, snacks were permitted. Everyone usually provided their own, although there were times when they were donated by someone with a big heart. The snack choice of your group depends on the preferences of the people in your group, length of travel time, and whether you're traveling during the day or night.

Restroom Breaks

Always visit the lavatory before boarding for departure. While in transit, take full advantage of planned restroom stops. While there are restrooms on the bus, they are reserved for special needs and emergencies only. Scheduled breaks were included in the itinerary to minimize restroom breaks, thus enhancing everyone's enjoyment. Taking advantage of these breaks, whether you feel it necessary or not minimizes unplanned restroom stops for the group.

Destinations

Our church also traveled as a group to a variety of other places. One such trip included a southern tour with three full buses that passed through Iowa, Missouri, and Arkansas, en route to our destination: Shreveport, Louisiana. Regardless of the size of the group and mode of transportation (auto, bus or plane), organization was key, whether with the church or the GBT Academy of the Arts. For additional examples of organized planning, here are some other places we had visited throughout the years.

- **Arkansas:** Bella Vista, Center Ridge, Conway, Hot Springs, Little Rock, Menifee, Pine Bluff, Russellville
- **California:** Los Angeles, Pacific Palisades, Riverside

- **Colorado:** Denver
- **Illinois:** Chicago
- **Iowa:** Davenport, Des Moines
- **Maryland:** Silver Spring (Radio One, TV One)
- **Michigan:** Ann Arbor, Detroit, Romulus
- **Missouri:** Branson, Carthage, Kansas City, Saint Louis
- **Ohio:** Cleveland, Columbus
- **Tennessee:** Memphis, Nashville
- **Virginia:** Middleburg
- **Washington, D.C.**
- **Wisconsin:** Milwaukee
- **Wyoming:** Casper, Cheyenne, Jackson Hole, Laramie

These trips opened the minds of many, giving them a broader perspective of the world in which we live. We are only as knowledgeable as we have made ourselves, and we should not assume everyone possesses the same knowledge. In one instance of travel, wet articles of clothing were brought on a trip, and their hotel roommate was exposed to clothing being laid around the room to dry! The explanation for this untimely occurrence was they did not get off work in time to finish their laundry before our departure. Again, this is where advanced planning and organization is applied. ***Prepare for winter in the summer.***

Itinerary

When creating the itinerary, decisions made included:

1. Determining the distance of the trip (stops, meals, approximate arrival time)
2. Age-appropriate Entertainment for bus travel (Movies, Games, etc.)
3. Planning places to visit once your group arrives at your destination. This includes time spent at each point of interest.

The following pages illustrate an actual itinerary compiled for an educational trip to Memphis, Tennessee, birthplace of rock 'n' roll and "Home of the Blues!"

Having previously visited Memphis and witnessing the rich history this city possessed, I thought, "How edifying it would be to share this experience with the church."

Our reservations were confirmed at the beautiful Peabody Hotel, famous for the March of the Peabody ducks. We visited the Lorraine Motel (the deathplace of Dr. Martin Luther King, Jr.), B.B. King's "King of the Blues," restaurant, and Graceland, home of Elvis Presley ("King of Rock 'n' Roll"). All these great "kings" had prominent influences and historical locations that were of interest there in Memphis. Included in our itinerary was a tour of the newly constructed Temple of Deliverance Church of God in Christ, which was pastored by the late Bishop Gilbert Earl Patterson. A beautiful sight to behold!! Just another manifestation of Gods continual blessing! Upon our return, a meeting was called to discuss with travelers what they had observed and took away. Suggestions were taken to incorporate what they had learned in our future presentations.

This bus trip provided an enriching opportunity to learn about these icons of American history. The subsequent itinerary will give more insight on these individuals with other well-known artists. A detailed amount of history of the city of Memphis, and surrounding cities and states traveled en route to destination, is included.

MEMPHIS
Home of the Blues
Birthplace of Rock 'n' Roll

Memphis shakes you. Memphis wakes you. Memphis moves you.

There's just something real about Memphis, Tennessee that gets inside you and makes you want to dance, laugh, think, or smile. Ask anybody who's been here. There's nowhere on earth quite like Memphis.

Greater Bethlehem Temple
Memphis Trip Itinerary

"Is that a pyramid on the Mississippi River? Indeed, why not—this, after all, is Memphis, named for the ancient Egyptian capital on the Nile. While pharaoh images and other ancient Egyptian artifacts have paraded through here in the renowned Wonders series of exhibitions, the modern-day Memphis is associated more closely with kings. B. B. King of blues fame, the King of Rock, Elvis Presley, and Dr. Martin Luther King Jr. If you haven't been to Memphis for awhile, you'll be surprised at its new vibrancy. Barbecue and blues are still big, but there's more."

Thursday, May 22, 2003

9:00 p.m.	Board Bus
10:00 p.m.	Bus Departs

Friday, May 23, 2003

10:00 a.m. – 12:00 p.m.	Breakfast
1:00 p.m. – 2:30 p.m.	Check-in at the Peabody Hotel

Peabody Hotel

Peabody Memphis

The Famous "Ducks"
The March of The Peabody Ducks, which is performed at **11am and 5pm each day**, 365 days a year, has been taking place for over 76 years in the Lobby of The Peabody Memphis.

For more than 130 years, The Peabody has welcomed with open arms both visitors and newcomers to this great city. From the famous Duck March in the Grand Lobby to the four award winning restaurants, the South's Grand Hotel has charmed its guests with unqualified luxury and true Southern hospitality. The Peabody's rich history is a product of long-standing tradition, change, growth, and of course, the wonderful guests. The Peabody offers a full range of services and facilities, including a fully equipped athletic club, styling salon, convention facilities, and catering services.

Peabody Memphis

- The hotel has 453 elegantly appointed guestrooms, 15 suites and 72,000 square feet of meeting space.
- 5-Star Rating
- Opened in 1924 and renovated 1981

3:00 p.m. – 5:00 p.m.   Tour of Temple of Deliverance C.O.G.I.C.

Temple of Deliverance Church of God in Christ

The exterior is a graceful blend of greenery, water fountains, glass, brick and stone rising up seamlessly to the lighted steeple and cross at the apex of the roof - more than 100 feet into the sky. Inside is seating for over 4,000 people in comfortable theatre style seats. The entrances and foyers are large enough to allow visiting before and after the services. The sound and audio systems are the latest that technology has to offer. There are two catwalks above the ceiling for special lighting and sound control.

THE SKILL OF ORGANIZATION   89

Biographical Sketch of Bishop G. E. Patterson

Bishop Gilbert Earl Patterson founded Temple of Deliverance in 1975 and twenty-five years later Temple of Deliverance Church of God in Christ has more than 13,000 members on roll with more than 6,000 active members. In May 1999, Bishop Patterson and Temple of Deliverance Church of God in Christ entered their New Worship Center which cost approximately 13 million dollars. Because the church has three facilities, it is described as "One church in three locations." On November 14, 2000, Bishop G. E. Patterson was elected as Presiding Bishop of the Church of God in Christ, Inc.

6:00 p.m. – 10:00 p.m.   Free time on Beale Street;
                           Dinner at Elvis Presley's Memphis

Beale Street

Beale Street has been playing the blues for more than half a century. Named after an unknown military hero in 1841, it acted as General Ulysses S. Grant's headquarters during the Civil War. But, Beale Street's heyday was in the 1920's, when the area took on a carnival atmosphere and gambling, drinking, prostitution, murder and voodoo thrived alongside the booming nightclubs, theaters, restaurants, stores, pawnshops and hot music. One club, The Monarch, was known as The Castle of Missing Men due to the fact that its gunshot victims and dead gamblers could be easily disposed of at the undertaker's place that shared their back alley.

In the early evenings, boxback suits and Stetson hats mingled with overalls. Young ladies began to sashay around and inside the bars, gamblers waited for an easy mark from the country to come strolling in, bug-eyed at the ways of the big city. If the mark escaped from the dice or the cards, maybe the rube would fall victim to Little Ora, who was always ready to prove her reputation as the best pickpocket between New Orleans and St. Louis. Or maybe he'd just stop over at PeeWee's and visit with the musicians, or play a little pool, or secure the voodoo protection of Mary the Wonder.

By mid-evening, the street would be packed and a one-block walk could take forever, especially if he had to detour around the medicine show set up in the little hole in the wall, or if he stopped and listened to the wandering bluesman playing for pennies and nickels. There was the sight of Machine Gun Kelly peddling bottled whiskey from a clothes basket back before he moved into the ranks of big-time crime. There were numerous gamblers setting a box next to the card table and sliding a share of the take into it for the church down the street. There were big vaudeville shows at the Palace and the Daisy, hot snoot sandwiches at the corner café jug bands playing down at the park and one block over on Gayoso there was a red-light district to rival New Orleans' Storyville. Good or bad - Beale Street created some memories.

The redevelopment of Beale Street is considered a catalyst in downtown Memphis' rebirth. In the late 1970's the City of Memphis bought nearly all of the properties along three blocks of Beale Street, and the Beale Street Management Corporation was formed with the charge of creating an entertainment district. In 1982, John Elkington and his company became involved in the redevelopment of Beale Street. Their primary responsibility was to focus on the marketing, leasing and property management of Beale Street in addition to developing the entertainment theme through the selection of tenants.

In 1983, the first club reopened on Beale, and one by one, clubs and businesses moved into renovated spaces, producing the most vibrant streetscape and activity center in downtown Memphis and the Mid-South. What was once all vacant property has turned into one of the hottest entertainment districts in the country. Over the past 20 years, the street has gone from the epitome of urban decay to the number one tourist attraction in the State of Tennessee.

Elvis Presley's Memphis - 126 Beale Street

The first full-service restaurant and entertainment facility to bear the legendary entertainer's name is located on historic Beale Street in Memphis, TN. The restaurant serves meals made from Elvis' mother's recipes and includes many of his favorite dishes on the menu. The 300-seat facility uses state-of-the-art sound, lighting, and video to highlight the musical performances live on stage as well as special videos produced especially for the club.

Located in the former Lansky Brothers clothing store, where Elvis often purchased his wardrobe in the early days of his career, Elvis Presley's Memphis provides patrons the opportunity to experience first hand the singer's personality through his musical and cultural roots. In every aspect, Elvis Presley's Memphis recalls its namesake's spirit and consummate sense of hospitality and showmanship, which earned Presley the title, "King of Rock 'n' Roll."

Saturday, May 24, 2003

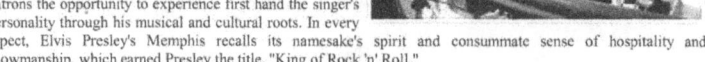

7:00 a.m. – 9:00 a.m.	Breakfast at the "Restaurant in the Alley"
10:15 a.m. – 1:15 p.m.	Platinum Tour of Graceland
1:15 p.m. – 3:00 p.m.	Free time and lunch at Graceland

Elvis Presley

Elvis Aaron Presley, in the humblest of circumstances, was born to Vernon and Gladys Presley in a two-room house in Tupelo, Mississippi on January 8, 1935. His twin brother, Jessie Garon, was stillborn, leaving Elvis to grow up as an only child. He and his parents moved to Memphis, Tennessee in 1948, and Elvis graduated from Humes High School there in 1953.

Elvis' musical influences were the pop and country music of the time, the gospel music he heard in church and at the all-night gospel sings he frequently attended, and the black R&B he absorbed on historic Beale Street as a Memphis teenager. In 1954, he began his singing career with the legendary Sun Records label in Memphis. In late 1955, his recording contract was sold to RCA Victor. By 1956, he was an international sensation. With a sound and style that uniquely combined his diverse musical influences and blurred and challenged the social and racial barriers of the time, he ushered in a whole new era of American music and popular culture.

He starred in 33 successful films, made history with his television appearances and specials, and knew great acclaim through his many, often record-breaking, live concert performances on tour and in Las Vegas. Globally, he has sold over one billion records, more than any other artist. His American sales have earned him gold, platinum or multi-platinum awards for 140 different albums and singles, far more than any other artist. Among his many awards and accolades were 14 Grammy nominations (3 wins) from the National Academy of Recording Arts & Sciences, the Grammy Lifetime Achievement Award, which he received at age 36, and his being named One of the Ten Outstanding Young Men of the Nation for 1970 by the United States Jaycees. Without any of the special privileges his celebrity status might have afforded him, he honorably served his country in the U.S. Army.

His talent, good looks, sensuality, charisma, and good humor endeared him to millions, as did the humility and human kindness he demonstrated throughout his life. Known the world over by his first name, he is regarded as one of the most important figures of twentieth century popular culture. Elvis died at his Memphis home, Graceland, on August 16, 1977.

Graceland Mansion

Just outside the ticket office is a shuttle to take guests across Elvis Presley Boulevard to enter Elvis' 14-acre estate. With the new digital audio guide featuring the voices of Lisa Marie and Elvis, guests enjoy a specially produced audio tour presentation and even more information on specific exhibits and items of interest. The mansion tour consists of the living room, music room, Elvis' parents' bedroom, the dining room, kitchen, TV room, pool room, and "jungle" den in the main house, and, behind the house, Elvis' racquetball building and his original business office. Recently opened was a section of the mansion that was previously closed to the public. The tour now includes never-before-seen items like the desk from Elvis' personal office and an extensive collection of his stage costumes. The highlight of the mansion tour is Elvis' trophy building, which houses his enormous collection of gold records and awards, along with an extensive display of career mementos, stage costumes, jewelry, photographs, and much more. The tour ends with a quiet visit to the Meditation Garden, where Elvis and members of his family have been laid to rest.

7:00 p.m. – 9:00 p.m.   Dinner at Isaac Hayes' Restaurant in
                             The Peabody Place

The Peabody Place

Peabody Place — the cornerstone of renaissance for downtown Memphis — is the largest mixed-use urban development in the South. The project covers 8 city blocks, with restored historic buildings, a 15-story modern office tower, classy apartments, prestigious offices, and popular restaurants and gathering places. In all, more than 2 million square feet connected by skywalks, corridors and trolley stations. Peabody Place is at the heart of a vibrant metropolitan area with 1.1 million residents. In addition, the city welcomes 8 million visitors a year, who spend $2 billion during their stay.

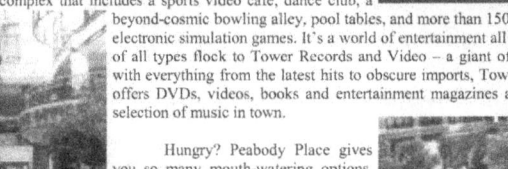

Start your adventure at Jillian's, a multi-dimensional food and entertainment complex that includes a sports video café, dance club, a beyond-cosmic bowling alley, pool tables, and more than 150 of the most advanced electronic simulation games. It's a world of entertainment all in itself. Music lovers of all types flock to Tower Records and Video – a giant of the industry. Packed with everything from the latest hits to obscure imports, Tower Records and Video offers DVDs, videos, books and entertainment magazines as well as the biggest selection of music in town.

Hungry? Peabody Place gives you so many mouth-watering options, the hardest thing is deciding which restaurant to choose. Like Isaac Hayes' own self-named restaurant, with tender ribs, soul food specialties and incredible live music. Puccini and Pasta gives Italian cuisine a whole new twist. There's Dan McGuinness Irish Pub, built from the ground up in Ireland and shipped to Memphis to recreate the décor, music, food, drinks and hospitality of an authentic Dublin pub. Fat Tuesday brings the tastes, sounds and celebrations of Mardi Gras alive every day. And don't forget the dining options of Jillian's.

Isaac Hayes

Isaac Hayes - Memphis

Born August 20 1942, in Covington, Tennessee, Hayes' formative years were spent playing piano and organ in various Memphis clubs. He fronted several groups, including Sir Isaac And The Doo-dads, the Teen Tones and Sir Calvin And His Swinging Cats. However, he achieved ultimate stardom with Shaft, a highly successful movie soundtrack released in 1971.

Isaac Hayes has finally blended his two lifelong passions: music and food. What that means for you is the best that the entertainment and food industry have to offer. Isaac is an accomplished Chef and the author of two cookbooks, and his flair for delicious mouth watering soul food can be found in every bite you savor.

6

Soul star and Memphis native Isaac Hayes lends his name and culinary skills to this restaurant/nightclub in downtown's new Peabody Place development. Live bands (soul, R&B, jazz) perform seven nights a week, and Hayes himself is expected to take the stage on occasion (hopefully more often than B. B. King appears at his namesake club). The food is a mixture of barbecue and Isaac's own recipes.

Sunday, May 25, 2003

7:00 a.m. – 9:00 a.m. Breakfast at the "Restaurant in the Alley"

10:00 a.m. – 1:30 p.m. Free time and lunch at Mud Island OR
Stax Museum of American Soul Music

Mud Island

A tribute to the majestic Mississippi River, the 52-acre Mud Island River Park displays the beauty and splendor of the river through the Mississippi River Museum and the River Walk, a five-block long scale model following its course from Cairo, Illinois, to the Gulf coast and New Orleans. The museum details 10,000 years of the river's history with exhibits. Learn about the shipping of cotton on the river and the musical history made in cities along the river, from New Orleans Jazz to Memphis Blues and Elvis. See the Memphis Belle, a historic WWII airplane. The amphitheater on the island hosts concerts in the summer. To get there, ride the monorail, featured in the Tom Cruise movie "The Firm."

Mud Island River Park has gift shops that offer a wide variety of merchandise ranging from Mississippi River related souvenirs to Elvis memorabilia. These stores offer merchandise directly related to the educational aspect of the Mississippi River Museum, publications and merchandise pertaining to Native Americans, riverboats, the Civil War and music of the region as well as decorative models, educational games, postcards and film.

Mud Island River Park has 3 food concession areas to purchase food: River Rest in the North Courtyard, River Center Deli in the main building, and Gulf Port Café located at the southern end of the River Walk. You'll find a variety of sandwiches, ice cream, snacks and beverages to satisfy those appetite cravings.

Stax Museum of American Soul Music

Stax Records is critical in American music history as it is one of the most popular soul music record labels ever—second only to Motown in sales and influence but first in **gritty, raw, stripped-down soul music**. In 15 years Stax placed over 167 hit songs in the top 100 on the pop charts and an astounding 243 hits in the top 100 R & B charts. Stax launched the careers of major pop soul stars Otis Redding, Sam & Dave, Carla & Rufus Thomas, Booker T. & the MGs, and '70s soul superstar Isaac Hayes, and Stax songs have become part of the pop music vernacular. "Green Onions," "Sittin' on the Dock of the Bay," "Soul Man," "I'll Take You There," "Hold On, I'm Comin'" and "Theme from Shaft" are classic radio staples that are instantly recognizable by music fans and casual listeners alike. While growing up during the

7

heyday of the Civil Rights movement of the 1960s, Stax was one of the most integrated companies of any kind as well as being the 5th largest African-American owned business in 1974. Stax outlasted most record labels—thriving from 1959-1975 and releasing an amazing number of lps and 45s—almost 300 lps and over 800 singles.

Soulsville, USA, is a small neighborhood just south of downtown Memphis, from where, arguably, the greatest number of influential musicians in the world have lived or recorded. The list of Rock 'N Roll Hall of Famers who come from this neighborhood includes **Maurice White (Earth, Wind, & Fire), Aretha Franklin, Elvis Presley (he went to church here!), Otis Redding, Wilson Pickett, Booker T. & the MGs, Sam & Dave, Al Green, & the Staple Singers**! All either recorded or lived in this neighborhood. Not a bad crew of musicians, indeed!

Other musical interest points in Soulsville include the birthplace of Aretha Franklin at 406 Lucy Ave. as well as her father's (Rev. C.L. Franklin) church, New Salem Missionary Church at 955 S. Fourth. Memphis Minnie lived just past Aretha Franklin at 1355 Adelaide. David Porter and Maurice White lived in the currently demolished LeMoyne Gardens, one of Memphis' toughest housing projects. Johnny Ace, when he lived at home in Memphis, lived at 899 Ferry Court, right behind the Stax Studios. James Alexander of the Bar-Kays grew up at 898 Stafford, and many of the Stax musicians rehearsed at his house before going into the studio. The Blackwood Bros. went to church at 1084 McLemore Ave. at the First Assembly of God(Elvis also worshipped here) one block east of the Stax Studios. And, of course, one of the earliest and most prolific gospel composers, Reverend Herbert Brewster, preached the gospel at Trigg Ave. Baptist Church 1189 Trigg Ave.

2:00 p.m. – 5:00 p.m.   Tour of the Civil Rights Museum (Lorraine Motel)

Lorraine Motel

On April 4, 1968, the Rev. Martin Luther King, Jr., was assassinated here at the Lorraine Hotel, just a day after speaking at the Mason Temple Church of God in Christ. Built in 1925, the Lorraine Hotel was a typical Southern hotel accessible only to whites in its early history. However, by the end of World War II, the Lorraine had become a black establishment which had among its early guests Cab Colloway, Count Basie, and other prominent jazz musicians, in addition to later celebrities such as Roy Campanella, Nat King Cole, and Aretha Franklin. Partly because of its historical importance to the black community of Memphis, Martin Luther King chose to stay at the Lorraine during the 1968 Memphis sanitation workers strike.

King, Abernathy, Andrew Young and other black leaders had come to Memphis to support 1,300 striking sanitation workers for an important civil rights struggle in 1968. Their grievances included unfair working conditions (on rainy days, black workers had to return home without pay while paid white supervisors remained on the job, and

THE SKILL OF ORGANIZATION

black workers were given only one uniform and no place in which to change clothes), and poor pay (the highest-paid black worker could not hope to earn more than $70 a week). Following a bloody confrontation between marching strikers and police, a court injunction had been issued banning further protests. King hoped their planned march would overturn the court injunction, but such plans were cut short on April 4, 1968 when an assassin shot and killed King on the balcony of King's room in the motel addition of the hotel. One immediate effect in Memphis was the end of the Sanitation Workers Strike with the recognition of the AFSCME union. Members of AFSCME now receive two paid holidays annually to celebrate the anniversaries of Dr. King's birth and death. In 1991, the Lorraine Hotel was converted into the National Civil Rights Museum.

7:00 p.m. – 9:00 p.m.   Dinner

Monday, May 26, 2003

5:00 a.m.   Board bus

6:00 a.m.   Bus leaves for St. Louis

Towns of Interest:
   Blytheville, AR
   Hayti, MO
   New Madrid, MO
   Cape Girardeau, MO

10:00 a.m. – 12:00 p.m.   Breakfast at Bob Evans & Shopping

Westfield shopping town northwest
Address: Lindbergh Blvd. & St. Charles Rock Rd., St. Ann, MO 63074
    St. Louis' largest Westfield Shopping town featuring Dillards, Famous-Barr and Sears, plus 160 specialty stores and restaurants including The Pasta House Co., Saint Louis Bread Company, Tilt Arcade and Entertainment Center and Wehrenberg nine-screen movie theatre.

12:00 p.m.   Bus leaves for Kansas City

Towns of Interest:
    Jefferson City, MO
    Columbia, MO

3:00 p.m. – 6:00 p.m.   Shopping & dinner in Kansas City

6:00 p.m.   Bus leaves for Omaha

9:00 p.m.   Arrive in Omaha

Planning Fundraisers

Fundraisers are an essential consideration of non-profit organizations. Internally, fundraising expands the church's allowance to create an additional avenue for proceeds needed to successfully serve the congregation and the community. Some of the essential components to a successful fundraising event entail:

1. **Brainstorming ideas** and getting input from participants to assist in thinking out-of-the-box.
2. **Having clear goals** including consideration of funds used in the previous year, in order to plan for the upcoming year's goals.
3. **Revisiting past successes** to learn from best practices and mistakes for future improvement.
4. **Rewarding valuable players.** All players are essential for making fundraising successful. The leaders, especially, help raise the bar of accomplishment by setting high goals.

While fundraising is an integral function to increase revenue, another important goal is to increase the fellowship and increase the involvement of church members. These two goals result in an ongoing cycle to support the development of the church.

Some fundraisers I have organized, directed and participated in include:

- Film festivals
- Bible notebooks
- Bake sales
- Candy sales
- Garage sales
- Nearly New Shop
- Waiter/waitress services
- Carryout dinners
- Septemberfest (Labor Day weekend carnival, serving as a food vendor)

As an extension of its community outreach, several events were held under the non-profit organization, GBT Academy of the Arts.

Some of our performances were held at highly prominent venues throughout the city of Omaha, such as:

- "Community Days" (sponsored by Younkers department store supporting local charities)
- CenturyLink Convention Center
- Holland Performing Arts Center
- KETV Channel 7
- Love's Jazz & Art Center
- Metropolitan Community College
- University of Nebraska at Omaha
- Wal-Mart
- Embassy Suites
- Hilton Hotel
- Marriott Hotel
- Red Lion Inn

Film Festivals: The nature of our church was one of merriment. We enjoyed entertaining and being entertained. One of many activities we sponsored was a film festival. The purpose of this activity was to visualize various topics in an educational manner, including historical and current events.

During our film festivals, we arranged the Dining Hall to simulate a movie theater. A large screen was set up and chairs were positioned for everyone's viewing pleasure. We even served popcorn and other treats to promote a theater atmosphere. Regardless of age, this event was enjoyed by all in attendance.

Bible Notebooks: Down through the years, we learned the importance of taking notes during Bible classes, saints meetings, and whenever a meeting was scheduled. The idea of selling notebooks as a fundraiser was discovered while attending a national convention. We successfully designed a prototype that would suffice for our use.

A select group of Pastor's Aide workers assembled the notebooks. Each page contained lines for a Subject, Title, Date, Speaker, and ample room for taking notes. Thus, we accomplished a two-fold purpose: to encourage note taking, and to generate revenue for our auxiliary as well as the church. This was long before tablets and smartphones were used as a means of notetaking.

Holiday Bake Sales: These bake sales provided opportunities to generate funds using outreach outside the church walls. Members of the congregation, including our youth, prepared an assortment of baked goods, which were then displayed for sale in an attractive manner, at public locations, typically small businesses and grocery stores.

These events provided an opportunity to teach cooking skills, sales techniques, and practicing professional customer service. This fundraiser was so tempting that a lot of the baked goods did not reach their scheduled destination. They were purchased by one another, and in some instances, individuals purchased their own baked goods.

Candy Sales: This fundraiser proved to be very successful. The candy was distributed to interested participants in the congregation, who then sold the goods to their family members, friends, and co-workers. This effort was especially popular with our youth, who always received an overwhelming response from supportive adults.

Nearly New and Consignment **Shop:** *This is undeniably a favorite of mine…buying, selling, and negotiating at garage sales, estate sales and consignment shops.* Quality for less is what you receive when buying and selling previously owned items.

The idea for a "nearly new shop" was inspired by observing another church which had a consignment shop I visited frequently. After seeking advice from those who oversaw this shop, I was encouraged to move forward with the process of starting a "quality for less" shop in my own church. The idea was accepted, and a decision was made. This would be another opportunity to raise funds for our church and offer fantastic bargains to the church family and community.

Our donated inventory included a variety of clothing items for men, women, and children, and the shop was open during regular business hours. Some did not care for the idea of wearing previously owned merchandise, but what they failed to realize is, even in the most renowned establishments, customers have tried on many of those items time and time again. Some have even been purchased, worn and returned. So, by turning down quality for less, we can deprive ourselves of real savings. Yes, pride has its place, but a penny saved is a penny earned. This kind of shopping has its advantages, especially when raising a family.

Not only did the church family purchase items, they also brought out their relatives and friends to shop. This endeavor proved to be a most enjoyable and profitable fundraiser. Despite some reservations early on, we had nearly 100% participation.

Waiter/Waitress Services: The idea for this fundraiser was brought to my attention by a fellow church member. She worked for a hospitality organization that was looking for additional waiters and waitresses to work at various locations throughout the city during the holiday season. After careful consideration, we assembled a group of interested, talented individuals to perform this service.

This line of work was not entirely new to most of us because we had performed these duties at numerous church functions throughout the years. The attire chosen for the ladies consisted of black slacks or skirts with white blouses, and the men wore black slacks and white shirts. The businesses were highly impressed not only with our manner of dress but with our promptness, performance, and efficiency. As a result, those companies we worked for referred us to other businesses that employed us long after the holiday season ended. We worked in many of the prominent hotels throughout the city, and we also served venues such as the Aksarben ballroom, and the Omaha Community Playhouse.

We were pleased with the results of our combined efforts. It proved to be an excellent fundraiser that gave these young people an opportunity to experience working in establishments to which they had never been exposed. So never say "no" to opportunities presented, as it may become beneficial to your **betterment** later in life.

Carryout Dinner: Let me begin by expressing that by no means was this fundraiser performed by only a few individuals. The Brotherhood Auxiliary appointed in charge of this fundraiser, nor the Missionary Auxiliary consisting of all the women in the church, nor the Youth Auxiliary, could have prepared and delivered over 3,000 dinners in this 12-hour period *alone*. This effort required the combined, church-wide commitment of all auxiliaries, including age appropriate youth. This dinner presented a learning opportunity for all ages to **better** understand how a team can work together to reach a common goal: a picture-perfect example of teamwork at its best!

We began preparing for the actual date of the dinner three-to-six months in advance. Teams of two or more were assembled to oversee each task involved. Calculating the amount of food and ingredients necessary to serve this number of individuals required careful planning to prevent purchasing more or less than necessary. Ordering the correct amounts of food was no easy task either. When the items were delivered, everything was counted and re-counted to ensure we received exactly what was ordered, and that all pre-ordered dinners could be filled.

Food preparation began as early as one week prior to the date of the dinner. Designated teams worked throughout the week leading up to the day of the dinner. Some teams worked without ceasing for 24 hours straight. We implemented rotating shifts to maintain this rigorous schedule, to successfully fill all orders by their requested times.

We also used teams of individuals to sell and deliver the dinners. This concept proved to be very successful. The competition between the teams to sell the most dinners, both at the team level and on an individual level, had more than tripled our total volume of sales.

Those who were successful sellers assisted in communicating the vision to those who were less confident. Team members would then begin working together to ensure all orders were delivered in a timely manner, and people who never thought they could sell soon found themselves exceeding their own expectations. This could only be achieved by a tremendous amount of teamwork.

> *Working together pays off;*
> *Working together paid off.*

Planning Weddings

Beginning the Fall of 1997, the church experienced a growth spurt, where the membership greatly increased, which subsequently led to wedding bells. Because there had come to be so many couples making plans to get married, a Wedding Committee was immediately formed. This committee was up and functioning in record time and proved to be very beneficial.

At the time I was charged with organizing this group, it was very time-consuming and perplexing. Everyone had their opinions as to how, when and where they wanted their weddings to be conducted. Often the bride, the groom, and family members voiced different opinions on many aspects of how the wedding should be performed. Final decisions made were acceptable if they were in accordance with the guidelines of the church.

Later, we organized subcommittees for wedding ceremonies, bridal showers, bachelor parties, receptions and decorations. A committee leader was chosen over each area, and within these committees were assistants working with the designated leader to ensure a smooth result.

Two-to-four weeks prior to the wedding, a shower was given for the bride-to-be by her Maid of Honor and bridal party. Friends and relatives gathered for the sole purpose of showering the bride with gifts. Games with questions and answers were designed based on teachings through marriage class (an ongoing session formed and taught by the Pastor. This class was implemented to better prepare dating and engaged couples for potential matrimony, and to further enlighten those who were already married.)

Food was prepared and served by the bridal party, family members and others who volunteered for the cause. Hors d'oeuvres such as cocktail wieners, Swedish meatballs, tuna and macaroni salads and fluffs, fruit plates, pizza, an array of dips and chips, and a variety of other specialty dishes were served. It was always interesting to find out what new appetizing recipes would be prepared. The parties were fun, educational and would lend to the opportunity of showing how much knowledge had been gained from attending marriage class.

The same type of setup was done by the groomsmen. They even prepared much of their own foods, but as the saying goes, "What would they do without the sisters?" The sisters usually would lend a hand in finalizing the men's party. Again, these parties are very beneficial not just for the bride-to-be and groom-to-be, but for all in attendance.

Immediately following the wedding ceremony, everyone would relocate to the Fellowship Hall where an approved menu had been prepared for the long-awaited festivities. The first order of business is the cutting of the cake by the bride and groom, with the photographer(s) selected to commemorate these special moments.

After the couple completed this wedding tradition, they were seated at a table prepared exclusively for them and the bridal party. The table is adorned in custom selected linens and matching decorations to coordinate with the color scheme.

These colors were not limited to decorations only; they also included the food. An example would be the fluffs with different colored marshmallows and homemade mints. Even the punch was colored to match!

With these meticulous preparations, the results were *breathtaking*!

Planning Funerals

Preparation for serving food at a funeral can be challenging. We purposefully prepared in abundance to ensure everyone was provided for, especially the families. A team of individuals worked before and during the funeral service to ensure the food was ready when the family returned from the interment. Warmers were used to keep the food at the desired temperature. We arranged a main table to serve as the focal point in the fellowship hall. Here, the bereaved family was seated. Other tables were set surrounding this main table; servers were then positioned and ready to assist where needed. The family was then served by waiters, while friends and acquaintances enjoyed a "buffet-style" dining experience. Once everyone was served, the family was offered take-out dinners for their convenience and enjoyment.

At its conclusion, after everyone had dined sufficiently, the committee in charge, which in nearly all cases consisted of church volunteers, commenced the clearing and cleaning of the dining room. Dishes and utensils were removed and carried to the kitchen to be washed, dried, and returned to their proper storage. Tables were broken down, and chairs stacked and stored. Dining room and kitchen floors were swept, vacuumed and cleaned within a reasonable amount of time. Everything was returned to its rightful place and ready for the next function.

Organizing the Choir

In addition to my general responsibilities to oversee each of the seven church auxiliaries and related committees, I was also tasked with developing a professional choir as the Executive Director. After many arduous rehearsals and constructive choir director meetings, the outcome was something the choir could all honestly look back on and remember as one of our greatest accomplishments.

While working to re-organize the GBT choir, the directors developed written documentation to support instructions that could be used to bring the choir to the next level. The following section describes what was required to implement standard policies and procedures within one segment of the church organization.

It is the responsibility of the lead choir director to oversee all areas of concern to ensure a productive choir. This reorganization required diligence in partnering with our lead director to help guide the directors and musicians and help perfect vocal parts, resulting in notable improvements in the choir's organizational structure.

Choir directors are involved in preparation for participation at councils and conventions. Each director assisted in preparing the training materials and handouts, presenting various components at each workshop, participating in role-playing demonstrations, and encouraging audience participation in activities.

The following job summaries were developed, showing the positions and related responsibilities implemented within our church, which you may or may not choose to incorporate, depending on the size of your congregation. These descriptions were developed based on the number of members and what each member's strengths brought to the Choir. In your church or organization, you may decide to re-align the responsibilities, depending on the unique skills of your team members.

Executive Director

Establishes and promotes a standard of excellence for the presentation and delivery of each performance. Evaluates and encourages enhancements of department functions, including the choir, musicians, directors, praise team, and administrative staff.

Lead Choir Director

Reinforces the established standards for development and direction of the choir, and its rules and regulations. Teaches, administers, and implements songs in accordance with the direction of the church's ministry. Leads the production and organization of programs and presentations related to the choir. Follows through to ensure program instructions are complete (i.e. brainstorming ways to implement the program theme and developing a supporting script).

Choir Directors (Section Leaders)

Assists with the development and direction of the Choir. Assists in conducting rehearsals and teaching section parts. Other duties as assigned.

Associate Choir Director (Finance)

Assists in conducting rehearsals, directing songs for services and presentations, providing written song lyrics, and regulating choir fees and dues.

Associate Choir Director (Robes)

Oversees the ordering and maintenance of choir robes. Enforces dress code standards. Maintains choir member information and the upkeep of the choir room.

Assistant Choir Directors

Assists with choir rehearsals, directs choir songs, helps with special projects, and other duties as assigned.

Minister of Music/Lead Organist

Communicates, delegates and implements instructions from the Lead Choir Director to the musicians. After learning the designated choir songs, instrumental parts are taught to supporting musicians. Assists directors with teaching section parts to the choir.

Musicians

Practices choir songs. Strives to be attentive to the sound of the other instruments. Follows instructions from the Minister of Music and Choir Directors. Also responsible for maintenance of instruments.

Director of Business Affairs/Organist

Maintains the purchases and care of designated musical instruments. Organizes records. Assists directors at rehearsals. Conducts outside business affairs on behalf of the Choir.

Creative Consultants

Supervises and assists with costumes and backdrop designs for special programs, flower arrangements and other decorative projects.

Announcers

Develops introductions for choir songs to enhance the congregation's understanding of the forthcoming musical selections. Delivers introductions with sincerity and enthusiasm to engage the audience.

In addition to directing, conducting rehearsals and teaching section parts, a choir director may also be tasked with the responsibility to perform a host of duties that maintain order within the choir. A choir director may be tasked with the responsibility to:

1. perform clerical functions
2. provide written song lyrics
3. develop scheduling of rehearsals and meetings
4. monitor the upkeep of the choir robes, instruments, and audio equipment
5. regulate choir dues and fees
6. help with special projects and "fundraisers"

Developing Leadership in the Choir

Engaging more individuals with the choir's mission in mind gives them responsibility and a stronger sense of belonging. Members fulfill additional duties for administrative and organizational projects. Communication problems were addressed through roundtable discussions on creative writing, publication design, editing and proofreading. Development was encouraged within the choir through seminars and workshops.

THE SKILL OF ORGANIZATION

Leadership is the quality that enables a person to influence others in a positive way. By networking and building relationships, a leader brings his or her team together to promote a common goal and recognizes the efforts of others. Some skills include the following:

- Continuously seek ways to improve your methods.
- Become technically and tactfully proficient.
- Promote the giving of feedback by allotting time for performance evaluation.
- Keep account of your members' actions while keeping track of delegated responsibility.
- Encourage teamwork by communicating and building rapport with each participant.
- Ensure completion of duties by providing clear directions.
- Make sound and timely decisions, with respect to the instructions and guidance given by your superior.

As leaders, we should set the example, be understanding, patient and accountable. It is important that we lead with an understanding heart when dealing with God's people. With leadership comes responsibility. Understand the importance of the job at hand.

Here is an excerpt submitted by the lead director of the choir:

> *A common statistic is that we learn and retain 90% of what we teach others. Therefore, by the directors being intricately involved in the weekly planning as well as preparation for local, statewide, and regional councils and the national conventions, they can **better** understand before sharing what is expected of them in their respective positions. These responsibilities also help the directors recognize and value the position of the Executive Director.*

Dr. Clinkscale also implemented fees to encourage punctuality and accountability among the members of the choir. Individuals were motivated to be accountable in their duties to become more mature choir members.

Throughout her pursuit in perfecting the Choir, Dr. Clinkscale has worked to develop greater potential in not only the directors and musicians, but also to improve the overall attitude of each choir member. However, as with any endeavor, there is always room for improvement. Dr. Clinkscale amply provided the Choir with the tools necessary to succeed under the anointing and to sing to the glory of God. It is the goal of the directors to implement the vision for the choir and to enforce the rules and regulations.

Tunese A. Goodwin, B. A.
Lead Choir Director

With the success of our efforts devoted to GBT's choir, I was then invited to co-produce alongside a choir director at the national level. Working with directors from across our region to coordinate 200+ invited choir members for this grand event in Shreveport, Louisiana, was undoubtedly one of our proudest moments. The performance received a standing ovation and even praises from the pulpit clergy.

These scriptures provide further guidance when operating in a leadership position whether with a choir or another type of organization.

But hast asked for thyself understanding to discern judgment. Behold, I have done according to thy words: lo, I have given thee a wise and an understanding heart.

I Kings 3:11–12

THE SKILL OF ORGANIZATION

But there is a spirit in man: and the inspiration of the Almighty giveth them understanding.
Job 32:8

My mouth shall speak of wisdom; and the meditation of my heart shall be of understanding.
Psalms 49:3

Wisdom resteth in the heart of him that hath understanding: but that which is in the mist of fools is made known.
Proverbs 14:33

Brethren, be not children in understanding: howbeit in malice be ye children, but in understanding be men.
I Corinthians 14:20

JESUS was and is about business. He created the world in a systematic order. He set the church in ORDER. Everything he does, he does decently and in ORDER. So, order IS in ORDER.
I Corinthians 14:40

Time Management

Managing your time is crucial when it comes to planning and organizing. *Psychology Today* describes time management as "the ability to plan and control how you spend the hours in your day to effectively accomplish your goals."

Usually a pattern of procrastination, which shows a lack of self-discipline, is brought on by mismanaging your time. Consistent procrastination develops a reputation as an irresponsible person who projects a character of being unreliable. However, people notice when you're practicing what you preach, such as when you're putting your life skills into practice by managing your time effectively.

> *A wise person does at once, what a fool does at last. Both do the same thing; only at different times.*
>
> Baltazar Gracian

On the other hand, learning to effectively manage your time builds your reputation, your dependability, and your individuality. People will accept more of what you propose when you acknowledge the importance of their time.

Those who respect you will understand when you have to say *no* to taking on more responsibilities than can be realized. Neither you nor anyone else has more than 24 hours in a day to accomplish your goals.

Breaking it Down

Break comprehensive goals into small, realistic steps. Use every available moment to move ahead and be productive. If you accomplish everything you set out to do on any given day, you will experience self-satisfaction. As the saying goes, "Not every day is good, but there is something good in every day."

Ecclesiastes 3:1-8 confirms these ideals on managing time and how there are predetermined ways to accomplish what we set out to do in our lives.

> *To everything there is a season, and a time to every purpose under the heaven: A time to be born, and a time to die; a time to plant, and a time to pluck up that which is planted;*
>
> *A time to kill, and a time to heal; a time to break down, and a time to build up; A time to weep, and a time to laugh; a time to mourn, and a time to dance; A time to cast away stones, and a time to gather stones together; a time to embrace, and a time to refrain from embracing;*

A time to get, and a time to lose; a time to keep, and a time to cast away; A time to rend, and a time to sew; a time to keep silence, and a time to speak; A time to love, and a time to hate; a time of war, and a time of peace.

Additional aspects of our lives, *as it relates to time management,* are non-negotiable based on your chosen career path. Your occupation, for instance, requires a set number of hours each day defined by your employer or the demands of your business, if you are self-employed. If you want to retain your employment, you will honor that time commitment and uphold your job responsibilities. Our life is on a timeline; the more we put into building a strong foundation, the more productive our lives will become. ***Don't put off until tomorrow what you can do today.***

Train Up a Child

> Train up a child in the way they should go, and when they grow old, they will not depart from it.

Proverbs 22:6

The object of teaching a child is to enable him to get along without his teacher.

Elbert Hubbard

Raising children to become productive members of society is another "non-negotiable" that requires time management and total commitment.

You cannot ignore the importance of teaching children how essential time management is to their whole development and their ability to thrive in the world in which we live. This process of training children is imperative to their eventual maturity. From feeding, changing, nurturing and the like, the schedule starts upon birth and must continue throughout their childhood and, in due course, their adult lives. Parenting is a lifelong obligation. Regardless of the age, you will always be their consultant, and ultimately the one on whom they can depend.

> *"And ye shall teach them your children, speaking of them when thou sittest in thine house, and when thou walkest by the way, when thou liest down, and when thou risest up."*
>
> Deuteronomy 11:19

Making Your To-Do List

There are many considerations for managing your time and making to-do lists. *(This is not an exact science and should be geared toward the individual.)* Determine HOW to spend your time by keeping activity logs. Should you choose to make a list, include all your desired accomplishments to make time for what you wish to achieve.

This list should be created as early as you like, perhaps as early as a week before, but definitely the night before. This will allow for an uninterrupted night's sleep knowing exactly where you will begin at the start of your day.

Bottom line: if you don't want to forget it, *write it down*, so you can concentrate on other items of importance. Making this a practice is especially helpful for when those ***senior moments ensue***. Keep on living, for as you mature, you will begin to understand this statement.

THE SKILL OF ORGANIZATION

When making to-do lists, remember to:

- Overestimate the time it will take to complete a task.
- Divide larger projects into smaller tasks with set deadlines.
- Be flexible and allow for interruptions and deviations.
- Know where you are in your plan and follow a set route when running errands.

This saves on time, energy, and fuel.

Depending on your generation, the days of using a pocket calendar and notebook may be a thing of the past. There are free mobile apps to help organize, prioritize and set reminders. Such apps include the Notes and Calendar software that now come standard with most mobile devices. However, if you are not up to date with modern technology, then write it down. Strive to keep all your checklists in one place, so as not to lose them.

In making use of an organizer, there is a myriad of organizers from which to choose; the challenge is to find the one that best meets your needs:

- Monthly calendars – general appointments and events.
- Weekly calendars – outlines the week in advance, allowing for more details.
- Daily calendars – lays out your day from the rising of the sun to the going down of the same and allows you to be more detailed in your daily assignments.
- Maximize your organizer by using it for more activities than just a calendar:
- Maintain records: keep names, contact information, locations, etc.
- Outline projects and tasks.
- Track deadlines and commitments.
- Keep detailed notes of meetings.
- Take full advantage of the convenience of smart phones.

Learn to Say No!

Learn to say "no" – not only to requests from others, but also to yourself. Doing so will curtail your distractions and interruptions. Setting boundaries and limitations on your commitments to others will enable you to stay focused on your schedule and achieve your daily goals. "Someday" is not a day of the week. If you want to accomplish your goals, complete your tasks after committing yourself to a due date (deadline).

Avoid unnecessary distractions such as excessive phone calls or checking emails and social media constantly. Limit these activities to designated times, so that more important activities always have time dedicated to them.

It is acceptable to break from your schedule occasionally, but don't lose track of what you need to accomplish on a regular basis. If you adhere to the schedule you set out to accomplish and the list of items to be completed, you will have a greater sense of achievement at the end of the day. Keeping appointments with yourself is just as important as keeping them with others.

Embracing a positive attitude will also save time and limit your distractions. Rather than entertaining negative thoughts such as "I don't think I can," or "It won't work," speak positive words. "Yes, I can." "I know I can." "It will work!" You must believe in yourself. This type of thinking will help you to push through procrastination, and mental blocks. In the end, it's a HUGE time saver!

A positive *attitude* can be achieved by having *gratitude*, resulting in a higher *altitude*. Be grateful for the small things in life, the blessings many people take for granted or consider insignificant, which can empower you to become more appreciative as your *good becomes **better**, and your **better** becomes your **best***.

When your *thoughts* become *conversations*, and your *conversations* become *actions*, they work to your benefit as your goals move to fruition. These thoughts are encouraging you to move forward.

This book first began as a thought in my mind, then I began discussing the idea with those close to me. Soon, the outline of the book became visible and I worked diligently over the next several months, researching, reading, writing, organizing, editing and proofing, until the finished product became the reality of what you now hold in your hands.

Thought to speech.

Speech to action.

Action to book.

Self-Discipline

"The individual who wants to reach the top in business must appreciate the might and force of habit. He must be quick to break those habits that can break him-and hasten to adopt those practices that will become the habits that help him achieve the success he desires"

J. Paul Getty

Self-discipline is the idea of educating oneself, which requires restraint and determination. In the minds of many great writers, this choice to discipline one's self is a key component to the makings of a successful person.

Your feet will never take you where your mind has never been.

Bill Winston

> *"Men are anxious to improve their circumstances but are unwilling to improve themselves; they therefore remain bound. The man who does not shrink from self-crucifixion can never fail to accomplish the object upon which his heart is set. This is true of earthly as of heavenly things. Even the man whose object is to acquire wealth must be prepared to make great personal sacrifices before he can accomplish hisobject; and how much more so he would realize a strong and well-poised life."*
>
> James Allen, author of As a Man Thinketh (1903)

Regardless of what you determine your mission or goal to be in life, it requires self-discipline. As Brian Tracy so eloquently stated, *"Persistence is **self-discipline in action**."* I had to practice disciplining myself to write this book. It required relentless dedication to a set number of days and times to complete my intended goal. When you begin to write, you strengthen your ability to remember to do what you have said. Your brain works in such a way as to bring your goals to reality when you write them down.

I wasn't sure I was going to accomplish this project, since this was my first mass publication. As I moved forward, it became evident I was becoming intrigued by the fact I was putting a portion of my life on paper. This process has impacted me in a myriad of ways, and although this project took considerably longer than I initially projected, the journey was well worth my effort. After persevering thus far, I am convinced the race is not to the swift, nor the battle to the strong, but to those who endure to the end. (Ecclesiastes 9:11, Matthew 24:13)

The sacrifices made by the members of GBT over the past 40 years in time, talents, resources and contributions were, without a doubt, the oil that kept the engine running and the blessings flowing.

> **The greater the sacrifice,
> the greater the blessing.**

...and the writing of this publication is one of the utmost blessings I achieved and received from sacrifices made at GBT.

> *A man's gift maketh room for him,
> and bringeth him before great men.*
>
> Proverbs 18:16

> *"Everything you want in life has a price connected to it. There is a price to pay if you want to make things **better**, a price to pay for leaving things as they are, a price for everything."*
>
> Harry Browne

Strive for Punctuality

Nurturing a habit of punctuality is an important part of self-discipline. Every culture has its own set of values and being time conscious is no exception. Arriving late for an appointment is usually viewed as showing a lack of respect toward others' time.

Have you heard the saying, *"Time is money?"* Wasted time is wasted money; therefore, if you have a reputation for being late, now is the time to strive for punctuality. Change how others perceive you by showing that you value their time as much as they value yours.

> *If you're early you're on time, if you're on time, you're late.
> And if you're late you're fired.*
>
> Oprah Winfrey

The world is designed around a basis of order. Organization leads to an efficient business. But organization and order are not available without a person to implement it and set it in action. This leads us into **The Skill of Leadership.**

Quotes on Planning/Organizing

Always plan ahead. It wasn't raining when Noah built the ark.

Richard Cushing

Planning is bringing the future into the present so that you can do something about it now.

Alan Lakein

A good plan is like a road map; it shows the final destination and usually the best way to get there.

Stanley Judd

Scriptures on Planning/Organizing

The heart of a man plans his way, but the Lord establishes his steps.

Proverbs 16:9

Prepare your work outside; get everything ready for yourself in the field, and after that build your house.

Proverbs 24:27

The plans of the diligent lead surely to abundance, but everyone who is hasty comes only to poverty.

Proverbs 21:5

CHAPTER III:

The Skill of Leadership

Empowerment, Vision, Example, Communication, Relationship, and Motivation

The Leadership Jigsaw, devised by Alan Cutler, highlights six elements of strong leadership. In the broadest sense of the word, a leader is someone who brings people together and guides them toward a common goal. Effective leadership requires more than simply the ability to delegate or assign tasks. Effective leaders can identify the strengths of each person in their group and who would be most successful in their positions. Recognizing and rearranging those positions may be necessary to communicate the vision.

Let's dig deeper into each one of these components and talk about how each applies to leadership through a few examples.

A leader Empowers others to reach their greater potential: 1) to give power or authority to: The administrator was empowered to sign certain contracts. 2) to enable; permit: The director led each actor to be more effective at their job by empowering them with the role to lead one scene per day.

A leader must be a Visionary: A person who has foresight or visions of unknown or future things. *the vision of a prophet; a man of great vision.* The prophet tells the congregation his vision of things to come.

A leader must set an Example: 1. A problem or exercise used to illustrate a principle or method. 2. one thing taken to show what others are like: New York is a world-class example of a busy American metropolis. It has tourist attractions such as live theatrical and operatic performances, and all the things you'd come to expect in an American city of its magnitude.

A leader understands the power of Communication: A giving and receiving of information…by speaking or writing. Ashley and Teia communicate every Friday through email about the script they've been writing together for the performance. Communication helps two people working together accomplish their goals together.

A leader builds supportive Relationships: A connection; the state or condition that exists between people or groups that deal with one another: Mark and Suzie had developed a mental relationship that was so strong, it made it a piece of cake to accomplish setting up the wedding they had been planning for just two months. Relationships often make accomplishing large-scale tasks easier.

THE SKILL OF LEADERSHIP

A leader understands how team members are motivated: The act or process of furnishing with an incentive or encouraged to act: The student is motivated by the standing ovations she receives from the class after reading off her submission to poetry club. When doing something difficult, being motivated to do it makes the task much easier.

---

*Not every reader is a leader,
but every leader must be a reader.*

President Harry S. Truman

*The function of leadership is to produce more leaders,
not more followers.*

Ralph Nader

A leader should:

Be creative – *artistic, original*

Be inventive – *imaginative, ingenious*

Be an energizer – *a booster, supporter*

Be detailed – *thorough, complete*

Be consistent – *reliable, dependable*

Be trustworthy – *truthful, honest*

Be an advocate – *an activist, promoter*

Be dedicated – *devoted, steadfast to the cause*

The Work Begins with You

The very first leadership position I held at GBT prior to being appointed Pastor's Aide Chairlady, was Chairperson of the Housing Committee. I made lodging arrangements for visiting members of the organization during regional conferences and other functions held in our city, placing them with hosting church members.

This position provided me an opportunity to interact with many other like believers. When families were placed in homes of volunteers, instead of accumulating hotel expenses, we could build long-lasting relationships as we fellowshipped with one another. If a family could offer monetary compensation to help with expenses, it was appreciated, but was never a requirement. I learned my first lesson in giving and receiving gratuity when a family stayed in my own home. Upon their departure, a monetary gift was left on the bed pillow of the room. At that time, I was young, and my travels were limited, so people leaving tips was unfamiliar to me. However, as time progressed, I've since learned the value of showing your appreciation – it is thoroughly appreciated.

These councils convened three times a year. Although my role as Chairperson of this committee proved to be of great value in many aspects, it involved a tremendous amount of work. Shortly thereafter, I realized how my responsibilities had increased even more when my pastor appointed me to the position of Pastor's Aide Director.

I have learned, whenever I am presented with a new responsibility, the work always begins with me. In the words of Michael Jackson, "It starts with the man in the mirror." This means being a leader by example.

*Leadership is not about titles, positions or flowcharts.
It is about one life influencing another.*

John C. Maxwell

When giving directions, it is important that the person you are instructing understands what is being asked of them. Oftentimes, things are done incorrectly because the message is not clearly relayed by the sender, nor understood by the receiver.

Never appear impatient! This could cause the one receiving the message to be distracted or hurried to a misguided conclusion in an attempt to carry out the instructions without a thorough understanding.

Directions should be spelled out and accompanied with an example whenever possible. Everyone does not learn simply by being told. Never assume that someone knows what you want. Their ideas and perceptions may be the total opposite of yours. For some, "a picture is worth a thousand words."

For example, when the State Mass Choir (combined choirs representing several churches) was preparing for the National Convention, the women were instructed to wear "tee-length" skirts. Some may have thought "tee-length" to be just below the knees, past the ankle, or to the floor. By explaining and demonstrating with an example, they all received clear instructions and could carry them out effectively.

Choosing Your Leaders

It is highly important that strong leadership be in place when starting a church, school, or any type of business, to ensure everything runs smoothly.

Confident leaders empower organizations and create a sense of purpose and order that encourages credibility to the overall mission and trustworthiness among its members.

An organized team is confident in their abilities; they have an advantage over unorganized teams. When an organized team comes together, they spend less time dealing with chaos, and are therefore able to spend more time accomplishing what they had intended.

Following is a compilation *(but certainly not an exhaustive list)* of characteristics that you will find in the most successful leaders.

1. ***A truly effective leader must have God's people at heart.*** Showing love requires a level of consciousness to understand others, and not just through words only, but also through actions. When love is demonstrated, it helps you to appreciate others, regardless of your differences.
2. ***Leaders are born, but undeveloped.*** With proper teaching and proper training, leaders will grow by degrees into a mature state.
3. ***Leaders are responsible.*** They take the initiative to act, make decisions and hold themselves accountable, and provide guidance and direction to complete the job.
4. ***Leaders are problem solvers.*** They have a positive attitude and, look for solutions to not only direct the flow of conversation toward positive outcomes, but also give positive solutions to help resolve complications that may arise.
5. ***Leaders have backbone.*** They possess strength of character and determination. They communicate the vision and implement the standards of unity and teamwork.

6. **Leaders realize they are not perfect.** Our tests and trials are learning tools which "worketh patience in us," bringing experience and hope.
7. *Leaders must win the people.* They must earn their trust and support by showing determination, and by being prayerful, positive, and productive.

Giving and Accepting Constructive Criticism

Criticism can be defined as judgments by a critic or a review expressing such judgments. Criticism comes in two different forms: *constructive and destructive.*

Constructive criticism focuses on what an individual needs to improve upon to become a *better* person. *Destructive* criticism focuses on belittling a person and contributes nothing to their self-esteem.

Accepting *constructive* criticism is usually difficult for most individuals. No one likes to be told they are wrong or lacking in character. If we take the suggestions given to us, we will learn from our mistakes and perform *better*. We must be able to separate our ideas from ourselves, otherwise we will become defensive, feeling we are not being accepted when, in fact, it's our idea that's being rejected. Accepting and applying constructive criticism will help us become more effective instruments for God.

When giving *constructive* criticism, always start by expressing a positive quality about the individual. This will help them be more receptive to what is being said. Beginning with negative observations tend to make the person defensive and not want to receive your advice. On the other hand, it may be more effective to start with the phrases "Let's try this," or "What was your observation?" "How would you have handled it?"

There are always alternatives in responding to adverse situations. (After all, we are among the greatest people on earth: God's people.) We all have the power within us to improve our own situations.

Preparation of Leaders

Preparation goes by a lot of alternative definitions. Preparation can mean:

- To sufficiently provide for.
- To forecast the unknown and look ahead to prevent unforeseen problems.
- To perfect an art before a performance. Rehearsal is imperative.
- To exercise and perfect a task, making oneself ready to achieve excellence. Practice makes perfect.
- To self-educate and increase in wisdom, knowledge and understanding on a topic.
- Build upon a set of skills to build a solid foundation
- To cultivate for a productive and fruitful harvest of increase.

Leaders look ahead in time to see and steer a collection of thoughts toward the group's overall victory. They prepare individuals to act to achieve a special purpose.

A leader also motivates people to actively achieve above what they feel they're capable. A leader is both an encourager and an interpreter. They often have a way of explaining things so that others can understand. Sometimes this advice is intentionally made easy for newcomers to grasp, so they can be "grafted in" and cultivated for fruitful production. This gives leaders yet another function: one who helps newcomers assimilate.

My experience at GBT brings back to mind an example I have of leaders preparing for newcomers to assimilate. After the "Amazing Holy Ghost Explosion," which occurred in the mid-nineties, numerous changes had to be made, when over two-hundred individuals came to the church seeking the Holy Ghost. Beginning with the first service at a council session, continuing through a series of events lasting approximately three weeks, they all had been filled with that precious gift. It was an amazing manifestation of God's promise in Acts 2:17,

And I will pour out of my spirit upon all flesh...

Out of the number of individuals that came to the church, the majority remained and became members of GBT. After such an overwhelming experience, preparations had to be made in order to accommodate all those newly filled souls.

The Pastor along with a committee of leaders responded by coming together to develop a plan of action. The Pastor used a statement similar to that which was stated by Moses in Numbers 11:14. Because of the overwhelming influx of people added to the church in that short span of time, he wondered what solution could be implemented in order to accommodate so many.

It was suggested that a book on church government be put in place. This book would include explanations and answers to the myriad of questions that are usually asked by newcomers.

In record time, the book was written, and a class was formed and functioning. It was established that each new member, as well as existing members, attend this class in order for all to be on one accord. This curriculum was designed to ensure that everyone knew and understood church protocol, namely what was expected of the church, and what the church represented.

Sometimes the Lord allows things to happen to take us to where we need to be. A book on church government had been in the making for a while, and this experience caused us to realize that this was the moment and time to bring this idea to realization.

Some ministers liken the church to a hospital, a place where the sick and brokenhearted can be healed. It is truly a place that offers opportunities and expectations of hope, and a place where love is demonstrated. If you're sick and in need of spiritual healing, love is the answer, for God is love.

> *Where there is a will, there is a way,*
> *and Love will find a way.*

Leaders are Mediators

Leaders are also mediators and equippers. Since members do not always agree on the path the group should take, there must be someone in position of authority who can settle differences. They take opposing ideas and mend them together into a concept amenable to everyone, and they re-equip the broken-hearted with a new spirit, preparing them to continue working with the group.

The Church greatly needs leadership that is inspired by our One True Leader. Success comes from following His Word, which was written aforetime for our learning. Good leadership requires that we carry out those principles in all the team's endeavors.

Preparation for Greatness

God has demonstrated the principles of preparation in His Word. Solomon in the book of Proverbs brings attention to how the ant makes certain of its survival. It keeps track of when seasons change and makes ready its meals in the summer, for when the time is right for gathering what will be necessary for winter.

> *There be four things which are little upon the earth, but they are exceeding wise. The ants are a people not strong, yet they prepare their meat in the summer.*
>
> Proverbs 30:24, 25

Just as these tiny creatures use their God given wisdom for their survival, so should we be as wise in preparing our lives for what lies ahead.

> *For we know not what tomorrow brings,*
> *therefore be ye also ready.*
> Matthew 24:44

Every leader, as the voice in the front of the room, has an opportunity to lift the spirits of their listeners in **preparation** of a great movement. In many places in the Bible, there were times when a great move was coming, and it was up to the leader to explain plainly the change, to prepare the people mentally and physically for greatness.

Moses was a leader of the people of Israel. He led approximately 2.4 million Hebrews in the Exodus. Before that, he was the leader of the Egyptians, imparting Pharaoh's will.

King David was the greatest warrior king. He united the people of Israel and led them to victory in battle. He later paved the way for his son Solomon to build the Holy Temple.

God's Word also speaks of how men ought to prepare themselves to work with others…

> *Two are better than one because they have a*
> *good reward for their labour.*
> Ecclesiastes 4:9

…indicating **teamwork**, which we will emphasize further in Chapter Seven. Sometimes the events are not the focus, but instead the person who's about to take new charge of the situation. The Scripture reminds us to take charge of our inner issues before stepping into a position, so that the Lord can make better use of us.

Without a doubt the start of a great season of blessings begins when the heart is **prepared to serve.** This brings to mind a time and place of Greater Beth-el Temple preparing for GREATNESS. A *great* move was about to ensue. After the purchase of a 33,000 square-foot church and school which sat on a 3-acre site, the word *great* does not seem *great* enough to describe a blessing of this *magnitude.*

I have undertaken many projects in my lifetime, but I had never envisioned an undertaking on a scale such as this.

I along with the head deacon of GBT, (referred to below as Deacon E. D.) was given by our pastor the responsibility of overseeing the renovation and restoration of this magnificent building. Since he was development section manager for the City of Omaha Planning Department for many years, his qualifications began to speak for themselves as the project initiated. How fitting that he would be given the title Construction Engineer. My experience in part being "life" (alongside my degree being Christian Education in Administration and Organization), I was assigned the position C.E.O., Chief Executive Officer, over Design and Development.

With little regard to the titles given, Deacon E. D. and I interacted as a team, beginning with sitting down with the architectural team and finalizing the building design, even to making decisions together on the type of windows to be installed.

Although I had been involved with remodeling, restoring, and redecorating in many other projects, including the project prior to the current church, none were ever as challenging as this.

Once the decision was made to purchase this property, I was taken aback by its size, not to mention the *inside* condition of this building. It was overwhelming to say the least. (– and I don't mean in a good way.) Even though the building itself was a diamond-in-the-rough, it required a tremendous amount of work within and without.

Our church had been prepared to go through two great moves that would redefine greatly the preparation for greatness.

Former GBT Renovation

As it happened, Randy J., my son and a member of GBT at that time and also a professional actor, donated his winnings of $20,000 from a simulated stock-car race he entered in 1997 in hopes of providing his favorite charity with the necessary funds to update its interiors. His only stipulation for us accepting this gift, was that we had to put a portion of the funds toward the remodeling of the church restrooms. This gift prompted the *great* church remodeling shortly thereafter, with the head deacon and I accepting the charge for bringing this project to its end.

With these funds, we were not only able to redo the restrooms, but also remodel the business office, the pastor's office, the nursery, and the nurse's station. In addition, we remodeled the entire lower level including the kitchen, choir room, fellowship hall, stage, and publication-office behind the stage. This included all areas of the church excluding the sanctuary—which had been done prior to this remodeling phase. 20 years ago, $20,000 would have gone a lot further than it would today, but, due to the efforts of all GBT members working together to achieve the goal of renovation, we made the money allocated go a lot further.

The investment and end result were well worth our efforts.

New GBT Restoration

Although the former church renovation was a *great undertaking*, what I'm about to share with you now is even *greater*. I am confident this is the reason the pastor felt *we, the people*, could carry out yet another massive undertaking: by renovating and restoring the *newly purchased Greater Bethel Temple*. In fact, that was his reply when I asked him if he was sure he wanted to move forward in the purchase of this building. His position was that, "[There are] enough people in the congregation, to whom God had given skills and talents, to do what would be required to bring this project to fruition. [We have] licensed electricians, plumbers, architects, consultants, commercial artists and civil engineers." Well – with much deliberation and some hesitation on my part – Deacon E. D. and I accepted the challenge. In 2011 we were able to proclaim, "It is finished!" "IT IS FINISHED!!!"

We purchased this historical structure in 2004. The original building project, Beth Israel synagogue, was built in 1951. The school wing was added ten years later in 1961. It was truly an historical landmark and undoubtedly built on a solid foundation. It had been beautifully finished outside in light, limestone brick.

The construction engineer accepted the task of refinishing and restoring the outside of this building to its original state. He had the entire parking lot resurfaced in new concrete and added a sidewalk to circle the entire building (allowing one to enter the building at any entrance, which made it very convenient for not only handicap accessibility but for everyone else.) Just as the members rallied to the cause of remodeling the former GBT, so too did they come to the aide of services needed in the restoration of the newly acquired GBT.

The construction engineer and I worked together to have the property completely enclosed with state of the art wrought-iron fencing. Trees as well as flowers and shrubbery of all species were planted, and new grass was sowed and laid. Retaining walls were replaced—some restored—and on the north side of the property, the grounds were built up and leveled, which literally required tons and tons of dirt being brought in to accommodate not only a playground but also garden space for the GBT Children's Academy. The completed landscaping was absolutely beautiful! We were more than pleased with the final result of the outside restoration and refurbishing of our building that would not only house the academies but also the new church.

In the building's north wing, we restored the school to house the Growing and Building Together Children's Academy on the lower level and Growing and Building Together Academy of the Arts on the upper level. In the south wing, the focal point and most significant area of the entire building was the church *sanctuary*, (my favorite,) adorned with its brand-new stained-glass windows—an idea taken from another church whose windows I had admired for years—and remodeled into a state-of-the-art worship facility. Another key component which adds to the beauty of the Sanctuary is the very large MURAL which was applied to the wall directly behind the pulpit/choir stand area. It is Awe-inspiring!

The baptismal pool was installed underneath the stage in the auditorium/fellowship hall, which was a unique way of housing a Baptismal pool at the time. The idea was to install cameras in the new fellowship hall and screens in the sanctuary to allow for baptisms to be viewed while they were being performed live, as it was the pastor's desire for everyone to observe the baptisms in action.

Continuing on the main level, we remodeled the kitchen and the dining hall, and a new nurses' station was installed. The business corridor, which included the pastor's office, the administrator's office, and other business offices, were also installed here. The new fellowship hall was partitioned off to include several rooms designated for Sunday-school classes and various uses. These rooms could be opened up by stowing away the sliding partitions, and then a full-fledged Auditorium/dining hall would be exposed. Many programs and functions all took place here. Dinner meals and other celebrations consisting of foods served in this space were "to die for." (indescribably delicious)

On the lower level, we restored the men's and women's restrooms, installed a nursery, and added a children's classroom, security office, and a choir room. A total of fourteen restrooms were either installed or remodeled (some of which housed four to six stalls, plus urinals). A massive undertaking indeed—but again, God had prepared us for this great move. The process of renovation and restoration **took seven years (yes seven years for the completion of the entire project).** Nonetheless with the many combined talents, generous hands, and creative minds all working together, we rejoiced to see that final day, which the Pastor had prophesied, come to fruition.

I firmly believe unless preparation is proven, God will not give you what you are not ready to receive. I give Him all the praise for the combined and wondrous works he had performed in our lives by allowing this magnificent work of art to unfold. Truly this was PREPARATION for GREATNESS at its best!!

> *But in a great house there are not only vessels of gold and of silver, but also of wood and of earth; and some to honour, and some to dishonour. If a man therefore purge himself from these, he shall be a vessel unto honour, sanctified, and meet for the master's use, and prepared unto every good work.*
>
> II Timothy 2:20, 21

Typically, the professional world places value on positions and titles. However, before being placed in a position, one should have prior knowledge and experience, proving their ability to perform. In some instances, a strong desire to learn is enough of a sign indicating a leader who is ready to be developed.

When assuming my appointment to pastor's aide chairperson at the former church, it raised my awareness of many changes which needed to be addressed throughout the church. By joining forces with the other auxiliary leaders and becoming acquainted with the various aspects of that church, I was also familiarizing myself with the protocols of these auxiliaries and committees. It made me very aware of a need to enlighten people on how to achieve a greater standard of living, while cultivating **a path to greater achievement within the church.** This education was self-motivating and led to my eventual elevation to church administrator overseeing these teams. It also encouraged my decision to further my post-secondary education in the coming years.

Leaders Stepping Up

In the books *Gifted Hands and Think Big*, Dr. Ben Carson shared how he successfully separated conjoined twins connected at the back of the head, being the first to perform this painstaking operation in a way that both twins survived. I was in awe of how Dr. Carson prayed asking for wisdom and understanding before each surgery. Through prayer and faith in God he triumphed.

Through continual prayer and abundant faith, I too sought wisdom and understanding to bring this book to fruition. Don't be afraid to step up and out of your comfort zone. Only you as a confident leader can make it happen. As you are now witnessing, God gave me the desire of my heart.

> *He is a rewarder of them that diligently seek Him.*
>
> Hebrews 11:6

It is my hope you can benefit from what we've discussed, even though your situation may require minor modifications to what we have suggested. Overall, traits of being a decisive, confident and considerate leader still apply though.

> *Every man also to whom God hath given riches and wealth, and hath given him power to eat thereof, and to take his portion, and to rejoice in his labour; this is the gift of God.*
>
> Ecclesiastes 5:19

We have discussed the importance of good leadership and benefits that can be observed when you have demonstrated it. The leader can become **better** by being a good listener and sincerely accepting feedback. This leads us into **The Skill of Listening**.

Leadership Quotes

Don't be afraid to give your best to what seemingly are small jobs. Every time you conquer one it makes you that much stronger. If you do the little jobs well, the big ones will tend to take care of themselves,

Dale Carnegie

Nothing ever comes to one that is worth having except as a result of hard work.

Booker T. Washington

A snowflake is one of God's most fragile creations but look what they can do when they stick together!

Vista M. Kelly

The man who views the world at 50 the same way he did at 20 has wasted 30 years of his life.

Muhammad Ali

Leadership Scriptures

*And let us not be weary in well doing:
for in due season we shall reap, if we faint not.*
Galatians 6:9

And I say unto you, Ask, and it shall be given you; seek, and ye shall find; knock, and it shall be opened unto you. For every one that asketh receiveth; and he that seeketh findeth; and to him that knocketh it shall be opened.
Luke 11:9,10

Therefore, my beloved brethren, be ye stedfast, unmoveable, always abounding in the work of the Lord, forasmuch as ye know that your labour is not in vain in the Lord.
1 Corinthians 15:58

Being confident of this very thing, that he which hath begun a good work in you will perform it until the day of Jesus Christ:
Philippians 1:6

CHAPTER IV:

The Skill of Listening

Can you hear me?

What have I said to you up to now?

Can you paraphrase anything I've said to you?

Can you quote something directly from this book?

What touched you the most?

Were you busy criticizing the book, or did you pay attention to its content? (Regardless, there is motivation in receiving constructive criticism.)

These are all questions pertaining to your ability to listen and gain an understanding.

Listening is not the same as hearing

First, let's define what the words "Hearing" and "Listening" really mean.

Hearing: *is the perception of the sound within which a voice can be heard. For example: I can hear the words being sung by the choir when the music is accompanying the choir and not overpowering it.*

Listening: *the act of hearing attentively, and the ability to accurately receive and interpret messages in the communication process. For example: When I listen to the choir, I'm intently listening for lyrics that I know will impact me personally.*

Listening involves a deeper desire to understand and involves being active in a conversation without having to say a word. Listening also involves being mature enough to forego trying your hardest to be right, in an effort to resolve a situation.

He that hath ears to hear, let him hear.
Matthew 11:15

So that thou incline thine ear unto wisdom, and apply thine heart to understanding;
Proverbs 2:2

Giving your undivided attention to the speaker can make a positive difference to what you will gain from hearing and listening.

Assessing your Listening Behavior

Let's take time to reflect on your listening skills, as these are the cornerstone of positive and productive relationships—both personally and professionally.

There are habits that can affect your ability to listen, and other people's *perception* of your ability to listen, some habits that you should avoid are:

- multi-tasking (watching television while studying)
- external noises and distractions (cell phones, loud music)
- a preoccupied or wandering mind (day dreaming, "Today is Friday."
- information overload (bombarded with too many projects)
- egotistical personality (overconfidence, "I got this, no need to study)

These habits can manifest into poor listening behaviors, such as:

Pretending to listen, which is technically called "pseudo listening"—where a person nods their head or utters something in agreement, but the brain is elsewhere, thinking about everything except what is being said.

Being a good listener involves being open to other's opinions while understanding what's important versus what's not important. You can use the information you need, and discard what you don't, but don't overlook the main idea the speaker is trying to convey.

Thinking ahead of other people's sentences, and thinking so far ahead of them, I assume what their opinion is before hearing it.

Assuming what the other person is going to say indicates you are **not listening** to **what** they are saying. It's hard to listen while you're anticipating your own response and judging without all the facts on the table.

This shows a lack of common courtesy, patience, and is a bit selfish.

> "...be swift to hear, slow to speak..."
>
> (James 1:19)

While avoiding bad habits, there are also good habits that can help you find favor in the eyes of your learners.

Sensing when the tone of the conversation changes and adapting to it, while maintaining eye-contact.

Even though your mind might be in a million places, your eyes should convey your intent to stay with the person in the room. Show interest with your facial expressions as well as with your body language. Make sure that the other person knows you care by the energy you express toward them. Listen with your eyes as well as your ears.

> ***Asking for clarification while someone is speaking, when you don't get the message the first time.***

Asking questions brings about a **better** understanding. If you don't ask, you won't know.

Do more than exist, **live**.

Do more than touch, **feel**.

Do more than look, **observe**.

Do more than read, **absorb**.

Do more than hear, **listen**.

Do more than listen, **understand**.

Do more than think, **ponder**.

Do more than talk, **say something**.
— John H. Rhoades

Learning Styles

Now that you have a **better** awareness of your listening behaviors, let's look at how your preferred learning style can impact your ability to listen to others.

As Director of the GBT Academy of the Arts, the need to incorporate a variety of teaching methods became abundantly clear over time. The academy was a performing-arts entity built on a strong educational background. The programs soon evolved into full-blown, artistic productions.

We incorporated entertainment through use of performing, and visual arts, as a unique way of taking common messages or ideas and implementing them in unconventional ways. The use of the performing arts appeals to the learning styles of people of various backgrounds. Applying the arts in these forms acts as a motivation for incorporating life skills. These artistic expressions proved to be a valuable aid in delivering a message.

Becoming a more effective listener involves being aware of your own learning style. There are several strategies for maximizing your learning abilities, and research has identified a few. Some researchers say there are *five* different styles. We will focus on three worth mentioning as they relate to listening: **visual**, **auditory**, and **tactile** (physical touch). Everyone is unique in how they learn, and typically have more than one preferred learning style.

Visual Learners

Individuals who possess a visual learning style can remember what they see, whether words or images. Using visual aids —such as pictures, charts, maps and graphs—increases this person's effectiveness in being able to listen. A visual learner should have a clear view of their speaker to see his or her body language and facial expressions. Here are some tips to help a visual learner grasp the concepts being taught.

1. Take notes while the speaker is speaking.
2. Utilize available handouts.
3. Make important text stand out using colored highlighters.
4. Illustrate your ideas as pictures, or brainstorm images.
5. Find areas that are quiet and conducive to only minimal visual disturbances.

Auditory Learners

Learning in the auditory sense means you absorb new information best when you 'hear what is said' as opposed to reading it. A planned speech, including the way each idea gets introduced and developed, helps an auditory learner absorb information. Below are more helpful tips for understanding how this type of learner relates to his material.

1. Read text aloud.
2. Create rhymes or mnemonics to help memorize.
3. Create catchy phrases or acronyms to increase memorization.
4. Dictate to someone while they write down your thoughts.
5. Use verbal analogies and storytelling to demonstrate your point.
6. Make speeches and presentations to reinforce what you have learned.

Tactile Learners

Tactile, or "hands on," learners are best engaged in listening when they are actively participating or physically interacting with their work. This means learning through *trial and error*. In carpentry, which involves working with your hands, most workers learn "on the job" how to operate their craft, often referred to as "on the job training." They are taught how to measure, saw, and hammer, by *doing it*.

Here are practical examples that demonstrate how a tactile learner might master a task.

1. If I told you how to ice skate, how helpful would that be if I didn't take you out on the ice and SHOW you? A tactile learner learns effectively out on the ice, not on the bench. Teaching a tactile person to ride a bike by riding it for them is ineffective. They learn how to ride a bike by riding it themselves!
2. Cooking is also best learned by being an active participant. In the kitchen, the more a tactile learner cooks, the **better** he or she becomes…and the more appreciative the family will be of their cooking!
3. In the military, you are shown how to make your bed… ONCE. Thereafter, you must practice until you get it right. In one branch of service, you're expected to tuck your sheets so tightly that a dime can bounce or spring back when it's dropped on the bed. One learns this only through practice.
4. A hair stylist learns the fundamentals of hair and chemicals *in the classroom*. To operate in a functional salon setting, they must learn the practical aspects by being "on the floor" with their hands in the hair. This practice includes learning to form pin curls and proper placement of rollers and manipulating the curling irons with confidence.

Additional Learning Styles

Solitary Learners

People who prefer to work independently and are inclined to self-study, are often referred to as solitary learners. Solitary learners are usually self-motivated.

Social Learners

Individuals with this learning style prefer interaction within a group or with another person. Giving opportunities to share ideas and experiences with others helps social learners to better retain information.

Verbal Learners

Preferring the use of precise words in speech promotes a more comprehensive style of learning for this type of individual. Scripting, audio recordings, role playing, and open discussions are key in assisting this learner in listening to and recalling messages.

Logical Learners

Someone who is a logical learner relies on rational thinking. Logical learners are stronger when the task to be learned involves working one step at a time toward a greater goal. The ability to think, understand, focus and analyze is necessary to this person's learning style. Reasoning, systems and logic are also key to this type of learner.

All four of these additional learning types tie back into our original story of the first three. These styles are simply accenting the first three types, as it is possible to be a logical, auditory learner with a tendency to listen and learn from voices around them, or, be a tactile, social learner who likes to actively participate with the group.

Regardless of what type of listeners we are, we all need to be cautious and pay attention to what's happening around us. Someone who is earnestly trying to learn has great respect for others' opinions. We all should learn to be open minded to new information which transforms us into being continuous learners.

Learn to Listen Responsively

Listening skills are beneficial in the workplace, as they increase customer satisfaction, productivity, and levels of information sharing among employees. Developing your listening skills is also valuable in your personal life. It enhances your self-esteem and confidence socially, academically and for overall well-being.

Children, in particular, are greatly impacted by whether they know they are being listened to by their parents or other important role models in their lives. As adults, we can easily become guilty of being distracted instead of giving children our undivided attention. These interactions can have long-lasting negative impact on a child's self-confidence if they are simply "heard" rather than listened to.

Conscious listening requires mental focus and making an effort to hear not only the words another person is saying, but also the complete message being communicated, along with its tone, its warmth, and all the positives and negatives.

Julian Treasure, who studies sound and teaches businesses how to use it, recommends the acronym *RASA*, which stands for

> ***Receive, Appreciate,***
> ***Summarize, Ask***

My interpretation of **RASA** is as follows:

Receive: take in the message alongside an understanding of the speaker's main points.

Appreciate: by gaining familiarity with the information being communicated, one can appreciate the message more.

Summarize: describe what would help tie together your understanding of the presentation.

Ask: develop follow-up questions to make sure you understood the message communicated.

> *Responsive listening is essential to hearing and understanding!*

Nonverbal messages

Effective listening requires that we hear and listen to both the words of a story, and the way it is told. This involves the use of interpreting nonverbal messages. Nonverbal messages utilize any of the following cues to create emphasis:

1. Tone of voice
2. Voice inflection
3. Pace of spoken words
4. Eye contact
5. Hand gestures
6. Body language
7. Visual aids

The spoken words may not always match the nonverbal cues. It takes an attentive eye and ear to pick up on what someone is trying to convey and to understand the message behind why a question was asked. It is important to note what is left unsaid or partially said.

"Smart" Listening

Being a good communicator involves knowing how to be a smart listener.

Consider what kind of learner a person is. If they are *auditory* learners, use the power of your voice to animate your presentation in a way that appeals to them. If they are *visual* learners, use a visual display to depict the details. If they are *tactile* learners, don't just tell them how to do it, show it by using an example.

Throughout this chapter, we have had an in-depth discussion about the science behind listening. Now that we've shared significant facts about the skill of listening, let's proceed with how we can improve our skill in speaking, as we discuss **The Skill of Communication**

Quotes for Listening and Hearing

Wisdom is the reward you get from a lifetime of listening when you'd have preferred to talk.
Doug Larsen

The art of effective listening is essential to clear communication, and clear communication is necessary to management success.
James Cash Penney

I remind myself every morning: Nothing I say this day will teach me anything. So if I'm going to learn, I must do it by listening.
Larry King

Children have never been very good at listening to their elders, but they have never failed to imitate them.
James A. Baldwin

If you make listening and observation your occupation you will gain much more than you can by talk
Robert Baden-Powell

Scriptures for Listening & Hearing

Bow down thine ear and hear the words of the wise, and apply thine heart unto my knowledge.
Proverbs 22:17

He that hath an ear, let him hear what the Spirit saith unto the churches.
Revelation 2:7

And he answered and said unto them, my mother and my brethren are these which hear the word of God, and do it.
Luke 8:21

Hear counsel, and receive instruction, that thou mayest be wise in thy latter end.
Proverbs 19:20

Take heed therefore how ye hear.
Luke 8:18

CHAPTER V:

The Skill of Communication

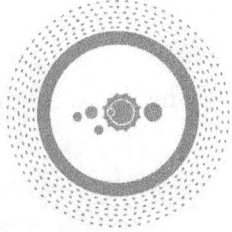

Basic communication

Communication consists of four elements:

- **Sender**: a person or thing that sends, transmits, or relays
- **Receiver**: a person who takes something that is offered
- **Medium**: a means of conveying something; *television and radio are a means of communication*
- **Message**: words sent from one person to another

There are three core types of communication:

Writing

Speaking

Listening

Historically, communication methods were limited to speaking, face-to-face conversation, the written word, and even visual aids like smoke signals, light signals, and hand signals. These methods later paved the way for telegraph and radio.

As knowledge increased, these channels greatly expanded to include the telephone, television, and electronic devices that can send and receive e-mails and text messages. These are just a few examples of technology employed in transmitting messages.

Today, there are classes, books, audiobooks and other methods of communication that teach how to speak and write in other languages. With the influx of the Latin culture in the United States, learning Spanish is beneficial to Americans in certain job markets as well as daily life.

Effective communication skills are essential to your success in all aspects of life. Many jobs require strong speaking skills that can help one introduce his platform. Effective communication is key to improving your interpersonal skills, and in addition, makes you more credible.

The Written Word

Learn the written word. Whether learning English, Spanish or even sign language, one of the first steps to writing and reading comprehension is knowing the alphabet.

The Spoken Word

Communication, no matter what language, is vital in interaction between human beings regardless of their gender, occupation, or location. If we cannot communicate, we are left in confusion.

The biblical story of the Tower of Babel tells how God changed the language of the people so they could not communicate,

> *And the whole earth was of one language,*
> *and of one speech...*
>
> Genesis 11:1-8

If we read closely, what these people truly needed and required was the collective idea to make the vision happen. When God saw how determined they were to succeed, He caused a communication barrier, changing the languages of the people so they could not communicate. This created confusion, preventing their attempt to build a city and a tower whose top may reach unto heaven. Language today is no longer a communication barrier. Modern man has established deep connections and cross-cultural relations, because of their ability to teach and learn new languages.

Listen Attentively

Communicating a message in a visual and verbal format to a larger audience can be very sensitive in nature. If the information is not heard and relayed correctly, the outcome can lead to miscommunication, causing misunderstanding and creating confusion. As emphasized earlier, when the Pastor communicated a message to the congregation, the members listened attentively. In particular, the planning committee members and I wanted to make sure what would be conveyed in our future presentations or demonstrations proved accurate.

GBT's programs and productions focused on using effective communication to reiterate main points from the spoken and written Word of God. The planning committee developed narration as an interpretative reflection to help apply concepts taught over the pulpit, while combining them with news and current events. This narration was carried out through the performing and visual arts, including songs, dances, stage plays, skits, costumes, stage designs, and bulletin boards, among many other means.

There's something truly special about bringing together writings by a variety of individuals, all motivated by the same purpose to compose artistic works together. When people of diverse backgrounds come together, they can bring a powerful message to the public that can change minds everywhere. However, to achieve a desired result, the message they focus on must be clearly understood by all involved.

Our church and arts academy developed several original speeches that were delivered to live audiences both locally and nationally. In some cases, this included impersonations and renditions of popular or historical figures, like Dr. Martin Luther King, Jr., Malcolm X, Frederick Douglass, Sammy Davis, Jr., Ray Charles, Stevie Wonder, Michael Jackson. Also included were Dolly Pardon, Whitney Houston, Mae West, Marilyn Monroe, Charlie Pride, Frank Sinatra, Shoji Tabuchi and Andy Williams, just to name a few.

Some questions to consider when developing a written message include:

- What is the focus of your message?
- What kind of appeal does your message have: personal (their emotions), professional (the formality of the job), or technical (the specific techniques one is to perform)?

- Is it for a large audience or small group?
- Is it for a formal or informal occasion?
- What do you predict will be the audience's response to your message?

Learn to communicate assertively

Assertiveness involves the act of having or showing a confident and strong personality. This means exhibiting confidence in the delivery of your message by speaking directly to the person (or audience) and making and holding eye contact. Displaying assertiveness helps to clearly communicate your intent.

Programs held for in-church functions or outside church all provided the need of helping each member practice using common courtesies with our guests. Our academy participants made a special effort to assert themselves in situations outside our comfort zones. We trained ourselves by engaging in professional communication with each other, so we were able to then go outside our walls and work in the field more effectively. Not only through our presentations, but also in our daily conversation, we enhanced our skills by actively practicing correct grammar.

Know the meaning of the words you choose to use. When you come across a new word, don't skip over it; look up the definition, and practice using it until the word becomes a natural part of your vocabulary. We carried out this strategy through teaching opportunities on proper English with our young people as well as adults. The children were provided these opportunities through Sunday School, and later GBT Academy of the Arts, and the GBT Children's Academy. These opportunities were valuable especially while preparing for functions, as we emphasized maintaining proper conduct throughout.

Stop, look and listen

Effective communication involves not only communicating clear messages, but also receiving the response from your audience. It is important to ask good questions that lead to answers useful for everyone. It is easy to become so focused on getting your message across or persuading others, that you don't tune in to potential messages being communicated from others.

Listening becomes even more critical in positions of authority. If your team members do not feel they are being given your undivided attention nor being heard objectively, they may not give the feedback needed or desired for overall progress.

Read between the lines. *Listen* and *hear* what is coming back at you so you can *respond* in kind. Look for nonverbal cues. Sometimes a person's body language, facial expressions, or breathing patterns, will tell you what you consciously need to know.

Body Language

Body language reveals much about a person, as it is usually consistent with true feelings. How we place our hands and arms, and even our posture in sitting or standing, can reveal our general demeanor.

Whenever speaking in front of the public, your body language factors greatly into how your message will be perceived. Exhibiting a smile, direct eye contact, nodding your head, or keeping your arms in an open stance can promote a positive attitude and reception of a message. Attitude can exhibit itself through body language, but body language can be misinterpreted as well.

These positions can also reflect a negative attitude. When we frown, slouch, fold our arms across our chest, turn from the speaker, or whisper to others, it can negatively impact the atmosphere. This type of behavior can be contagious and influence others.

Therefore, it is important to be mindful of how strictly you judge others. It is important to be mindful of your own actions and body language to minimize misinterpretation by others.

> *What you see is not always what you think you see.*

Three Effective Communication Strategies

As we tie together the particulars described thus far, there are three communication strategies you can implement in your approach to conversations. Each of these approaches becomes useful in their own specific situations. Mastering the art of choosing the right strategy can make your conversations have lasting impact.

Strategy 1: Thoroughly understand the communication process

Understand the basics of your message

When you are the "sender" initiating a message, you have the responsibility to relay information to someone else. Your first job should be to understand the elements of that message. The foundation of your message should be based on facts. Keep it concise. Everyone's time ought to be considered valuable, so you should know what you want to say ahead of time and stick to the point.

Breathe deeply and slowly to calm nerves about the situation. Use pauses thoughtfully throughout your conversations or presentations to convey emotion and important ideas. Do whatever you can to make it clear to the "receiver" their attention to those key details is what matters.

It takes time to absorb new information.

Recognize disruptive factors

Problems can arise when speakers fail to recognize the importance of the overall demeanor of the audience when speaking or giving a performance.

No matter who has the pleasure of receiving your message, they are bound to have pre-conceptions, which are sometimes misconceptions, and your job is to remain accepting but on task with your purpose. Keep an open mind to ideas from your receivers. If they have feedback to give you after the presentation, be open to the discussion.

There are numerous kinds of nonverbal cues the receiver can send you, including laughter, side-chatter, blushing, and the like. If your audience seems disengaged, try a different approach. Sometimes only a few more words, said in a different way, will help get someone back on track. However, if people become overwhelmed by a situation, then it may be time to take a break. Sometimes regrouping can make all the difference in our attitudes. There is a time to speak, and a time to refrain from speaking.

It takes two people to argue, but as the speaker you must rise to a level above argument to appease people. Don't provoke any situation that may already be fueled by passion. If you reciprocate their tone of voice and come back at someone on their level, you may fuel emotions and end up disengaging the rest of the audience. It recalls an old saying, "It's a fool that argues with himself."

Seek to improve future conversations by asking for and listening to a response on how well your message was received. Remember that the ranking of how well you have done is heavily dependent on how well your audience understands. Being on one accord with your receiver indicates a job well done. Achieving this milestone is priceless.

Strategy 2:
Send clear and concise messages

Once common ground is established, the goal of the speaker should be to maintain a clear focus on the message and maintain a flow from start to finish (continuity) throughout the message.

You don't have to be a walking dictionary to respectfully address your audience. It's not good to "talk down" to them or use words with which they are unfamiliar. As much as possible, identify with the audience, and ensure the entire audience understands the message you're trying to relay.

The appropriate words

Choose your words carefully, noting the flow of the conversation. Avoid being too vague. Though your goal may be to prove a point, conveying that point in the most tangible way possible requires that you understand what words make the most sense for your situation.

Supportive, nonverbal cues

Be consistent with your demeanor throughout your conversation, conveying emotion through each word you speak. Done properly, your receiver will then be able to tell you're invested in *them*, and they will likely respond more openly.

Let the words of my mouth,
and the meditation of my heart,
be acceptable in thy sight.

Psalm 19:14

The communication method

When having a face-to-face conversation, take full advantage of having access to all verbal and nonverbal cues coming from your receiver. Present yourself in a professional manner. Meet your peers at first glance with eye contact and perhaps a handshake, hug or warm greeting.

As for written conversation, keep your initial email communication or text message short and precise. If you're sending instructions, follow up with your receiver to add more details as necessary for clarity. If your written discussion involves someone else, copy those individuals on all email messages exchanged. Contact the individuals beforehand to make them aware of the forthcoming messages.

One of the most important things becomes how you speak, and your tone of voice. If you have a lack of sincerity or enthusiasm conveyed through your voice, you might lose a person's attention. On the other hand, as the conversation will not be able to be replayed later unless it is being taped, make every attempt to speak clearly, while stopping to elaborate when you want to make something stand out.

Consider diversity factors

Keep in mind when speaking to another person, their background is uniquely theirs. To minimize the potential for making blind assumptions, be mindful of whether you're acting in good taste to avoid offending people on standards of ethnicity, race, generation, culture or religion. Do not let an offending or distasteful comment drive a wedge between you and your receiver by the end of the conversation.

Strategy 3:
Actively Seek to Understand

A speaker must develop the ability to listen for context clues that help discern when there is a miscommunication. You can then develop a keen sense of how to get the conversation back on track.

Here are ways to convey a mutually meaningful message.

Effective listening skills

Treat your listener with respect by sincerely listening to what they have to say. Likewise, be receptive to your receiver's opinions. It can help you both remain on the same wavelength.

Being sensitive is not "being soft" or being a pushover type—being sensitive helps you respond sincerely to what someone else is saying. It also helps communicate that you are taking their time and their thoughts seriously.

Ask clarifying questions

Often when we get so caught up in making our voice heard, we focus on what we understand, but neglect to mention when we don't understand something. Even leaders can enter conversations with their superiors and followers without obtaining a complete understanding. Ask sincere, leading questions that get your receivers to offer additional facts. You never know—the answers you get may be the key to saving the conversation.

Ask questions to get information. Some questions you ask will probably be designed to test whether your listener understands you clearly. But don't overdo it—some questions can make other people feel undervalued or berated when you do not mean to do so. To avoid this, think questions out ahead of time.

Finally, advise out of love. Be honest and considerate, so that you, can be on the same page and end on one accord.

Making a Connection

Mastering the art of communication comes with the benefit of seeing your listeners leave with a clearer understanding of different points of view. If you consciously keep these thoughts we've talked about in mind, it can help develop your ability to perform at any moment's notice.

This leads us into the practice of making public speeches and appearances, in **The Skill of Making Your Presentation.**

Quotes on Communication

Communication is a skill you can learn. It's like riding a bicycle or typing. If you work at it, you can rapidly improve the quality of every part of your life.

Brian Tracy

Write to be Understood, Speak to be Heard, Read to Grow.

Lawrence Clark Powell

Music is the greatest communication in the world. Even if people don't understand the language that you're singing in, they still know good music when they hear it.

Lou Rawls

Wise men speak because they have something to say; Fools because they have to say something.

Plato

Scriptures on Communication

Let no corrupt communication proceed out of your mouth, but that which is good to the use of edifying, that it may minister grace unto the hearers.

Ephesians 4:29

For by thy words thou shalt be justified, and by thy words thou shalt be condemned.

Matthew 12:37

A fool uttereth all his mind: but a wise man keepeth it in till afterwards.

Proverbs 29:11

Let your speech be alway with grace, seasoned with salt, that ye may know how ye ought to answer every man.

Colossians 4:6

He that answereth a matter before he heareth it, it is folly and shame unto him.

Proverbs 18:13

CHAPTER VI:

The Skill of Making Your Presentation

How well anything is presented determines how well it is received.

Effective communication through presentation can impact a variety of audiences such as communities, organizations, schools, and churches.

Dr. Martin Luther King, Jr.'s "I Have a Dream Speech" is widely heralded as one of our nation's most renowned speeches of all time. The "March on Washington," which occurred August 28, 1963, was the largest demonstration ever organized in our nation's capital and brought over 250,000 citizens to the Lincoln Memorial to advocate for the civil and economic rights of African Americans. The message delivered by Dr. King truly did resonate with the audience and resonates in the hearts of many Americans even to this day.

If you deliver a message that resonates with your audience and motivates them, it will likely be instilled in their hearts and internalized in their future behavior.

Just as I have made each presentation "my own", you must tailor your ideas and make them suitable to your organization's mission. Proper planning and preparation results in a successful presentation. An effective presentation requires preparation by devising a plan, practicing, then presenting. There are several characteristics needed to produce worthy, sincere presentations, and knowing what those are is essential to your success. What will set you apart from everyone else is your appearance, your attitude, and your attention to detail. Most importantly, your ability to convince people that you genuinely care, will compel them to remember who you are.

ENUNCIATE. To mutter or mumble annoys an audience. A speaker who does not speak clearly into the provided microphone and reads without giving eye contact will lose the interest of the audience. One way to check whether you are speaking clearly is to record yourself. You can also practice your presentation in front of a mirror.

> *Be proud of yourself (but not conceited),*
> *of who you are, of what you do, of where you work.*
> *Don't apologize for your station in life or for yourself.*
> *You are what you are—so handle yourself with*
> *pride and respect.*
>
> Les Giblin

Animating Your Audience

When communicating with your audience you need to be *animated!* This doesn't mean being excessive with your actions and expressions (attempting to be a standup comedian, or overly expressive in your presentation), but being precise in your movements, your body language, and your intonation. You need to be able to keep your audience from dozing off or wondering why they are there. Therefore, developing the ability to "animate your audience" is vital.

Animation:

The act, process, or result of imparting life, interest, spirit, motion, or activity; To make lively or vigorous; To enliven.

You are animating your presentation when you are rousing, stimulating, stirring up, and bringing the audience to life. Images that are easily recognized can put your audience at ease and differentiate you as a real, caring, and trustworthy person. They can also impress upon others how relatable and accessible you can be to them. When people come to hear someone speak, the assumption is that the speaker is knowledgeable and sincere. You don't want people to see you as conceited or 'full of yourself.'

Being lighthearted, observant, and diversified in the delivery of your presentation, will make a lasting impression. There are many things you can do to make your act your own. Taking a common message or idea and implementing it in an unconventional way is simply being creative.

> "First impressions are sometimes lasting impressions, but a first impression could be your last impression."
> Randy J. Goodwin

Preparing your Presentation

We give useful practical pointers to help you prepare for giving an excellent address.

Voice Production and Body Language:

- How one displays thoughts and feelings through gestures, facial expressions, and movements of the body is key during a presentation.
- Speaking, tone, inflections, pace, and volume, can tell a lot about a person, including if they are confident/ timid, informed/unsure, or searching/ covering up.

Appealing to the Audience (Why They Should Heed):

- Because the presenter, not just the presentation, is interesting and engaging. The speaker is knowledgeable, thorough, audible, confident!

Design and Delivery of a Presentation:

- We are building your presentation from the ground up. Everything you learn through this book lends to better designing and delivering of your presentation.

Rehearsing:

- You may have heard the saying: "Practice makes perfect." In other words, you can perfect your art through practice, and be flawless in your presentation. Go over your material multiple times. MEMORIZE as much as possible.
- Go over your presentation until you know your expressions and intonations of how you speak, and when you want to put emphasis on something.

Nerves and Anxiety:

- Convert your nervous energy into vitality and enthusiasm. Do breathing exercises and/or stretches to loosen the tension in the body. Get plenty of rest and know your material before making your presentation.

Style and Techniques

- Be creative with your presentations. Use props, skits and diversity. Research successful techniques used by other speakers.

Building Confidence

- Greet the people attending your speech, class, or meeting, as they arrive. Briefly introduce yourself on a genuine level. You'll be amazed at how willing people are to open up when they feel comfortable. Be real. It's much easier to speak in the way you would with a group of friends than strangers.
- Use positive words and affirmations with your audience. Reiterating "You can!" builds confidence among attendees.

Following these few steps can make the difference between what is mediocre and what could be considered as excellent.

Creative Presentation Skills

Brainstorming innovative ways to creatively present yourself can be an enjoyable learning process. Being creative allows you to be innovative, to showcase your uniqueness and stand out as a visionary.

Make your version of creativity your personal stamp—whatever you choose to do. Putting your personal "stamp," or signature, on a performance helps build a brand that is uniquely yours. People will become familiar with your stage manner, your style of speaking, and elect to follow accordingly. Bringing a unique level of excitement to the stage helps the audience lock in an image of what to expect when they see a performance or hear you speaking.

Along with the planning committee, we combined current events with recent messages from the office of the pastor in visually creative ways to share with the audience. Taking time to work through this creative process made for an entertaining and enlightening presentation. Thus, after a period of time, the GBT Academy of the Arts was formed to extend our community outreach. The Academy received rave reviews, locally and nationally, because of these artistic presentations.

Presentation Set-Ups

There are countless ways to set up for a presentation, depending on the occasion as well as the location. Due to limited space and also its convenience, we would use the old (former) church sanctuary when doing fundraising campaigns for the congregation and for award ceremonies. For other setups we had various rooms in addition to the fellowship hall depending on what worked best:

- For seminars or saints meeting classes, we would use the fellowship hall.
- For a class session, the seating in the fellowship hall would be arranged in a C- or half-moon shape.

- For movie nights, theater-style seating was used with rows of chairs facing the stage, including three aisles: an open center aisle and two on the outer sides of the room.

There were also times when the entire fellowship hall was not needed. When this occurred, we used partitions to section off a portion of the room, then chairs and tables were arranged for the occasion.

An example of a pertinent use of partitions was GBT's Valentine's Day Celebration. We organized a Valentine's Day celebration for all the single ladies. Yes, all the single ladies! There were approximately 60 women in attendance, including the assistants. Hors d'oeuvres were served, and gifts were presented to the honorees. Tables and seating were in a horseshoe setting with presentations made from the center opening where all could see clearly.

The fellowship hall stage was used for computer classes and partitioned off for privacy. Classrooms could be used for multiple purposes. One room was given the name multi-purpose room, where not only classes, but also presentations and a variety of other activities, were held. Another classroom was set up with tables where commercial plastic wrap had been applied to protect the carpeted floors, where a portion of the food for the carryout dinners would be prepared.

We also had a spacious room transformed to fulfill any given purpose at any given time. It was used as a choir room, Sunday-school classroom, or marketing room.

My folks always said, "Use your head for more than a hat rack!" I tried to do just that. Where there is a will, there is a way…and love will motivate, provoke and inspire one to find a way. Creative minds can work wonders.

Goodwill Presentations

We presented multiple types of goodwill presentations, giving honor where honor was due. Honoring and celebrating others is one of my favorite and utmost heartfelt activities. I thoroughly enjoy making people feel good about themselves, encouraging them to do better, to move forward, and to increase in understanding, wisdom and knowledge.

Goodwill can be defined as exhibiting a friendly, helpful, or cooperative attitude. Similar words include compassion, goodness, kindness, consideration, and charity. Showing charity (love) towards others can be demonstrated by making presentations of goodwill. The following scripture supports this idea of goodwill in describing how it can be manifested:

> *Render therefore to all their dues: tribute to whom*
> *tribute is due; custom to whom custom;*
> *fear to whom fear; honour to whom honour.*
>
> Romans 13:7

Training sessions

Long before the purchase of the new church, we began holding numerous training sessions on how to best give a presentation, such as how to conduct oneself in front of an audience. Some of the trainings included "Projecting Your Voice," "Speech Delivery," "Selling Yourself to the Audience," and "Managing Time on Stage." These training sessions served a two-fold purpose of encouraging both stage skills, and the confidence to use them.

Self-improvement sessions

Most of us are seeking ways of improvement. After all, most of us want to do *better*, be *better*, and become the best we can be. We just need encouragement in how this can be accomplished. This is referred to as "image building."

Public speaking is one of the most common fears and causes for anxiety, but you can choose to face your fears head on. With practice, they will lessen, and you will become a *better* speaker.

Motivational Presentations

The presentations given at GBT, and the GBT Academy, regardless of the topics presented, were all primarily motivational. Our intentions were to provoke our participants unto good works—and to encourage them to do their very best in their performances.

Writing Your Speech

Barack Hussein Obama was the first African-American elected to the office of President of the United States.

- He successfully completed two, four-year terms (2008–2016).
- He declined 84 million dollars in public funds, instead receiving donations from his proud supporters who came out in record numbers to vote on election day.
- The provisions in the Affordable Care Act signed 2010, most notably known as Obamacare, have been reported to be the most significant changes to national healthcare since Medicare.
- He attracted record-breaking numbers of attendees in Washington, D.C., at his inauguration acceptance speech in 2008.

The speeches of the 44th President of the United States, whether written himself or dictated by him and written by someone else, were always planned out and reflected his unique voice. You, too, should follow an outline to deliver a speech. As you are speaking, stay true to your purpose to inform, demonstrate, or motivate.

When outlining your presentation, have a clearly defined introduction, with an attention-getting statement at the beginning. The introduction should share the subject of your speech, how it will benefit your audience, and what your level of expertise is on the subject.

Throughout your presentation, remember to use concise words and sentences that will appeal to your listeners. Limit your speech to avoid covering too many points and provide specific examples or stories that relate.

End with a strong conclusion that not only reiterates your main points, but also leave your audience with a thought for future action and time for potential questions.

Thinking outside the box

Presenting a topic in a unique way is key to making your speech more impactful. Incorporating slideshows or PowerPoint presentations, as well as multiple presenters, can make it much more interesting. For my doctoral dissertation, "Implementing the Mind of the Pastor in the Church," I created a PowerPoint presentation, that included three of my assistants who aided in the presenting of the material. This made for a more engaging outcome which brought supportive comments and praise from the members on the judging panel.

The development process of my dissertation was lengthy, requiring several months of preparation and rework. When you are working intently on a subject, it is possible to become complacent unless you continuously develop innovative ways to better refine your intended result: **the final presentation**. The hard work will pay off. Work hard to make your final product easy for your audience to relate to and enjoy. This involves taking time to reflect on how you can engage others in some of your finer points, and it takes looking at things from multiple points of view to get this right. Doing this is what makes your work memorable, and it solidifies your image.

I implore you to always look for ways to think outside the box and be creative.

The Three V's for Presentation

It's been said by many authors that there are three elements that all make up the effort you put into your presentation: The Visual, The Verbal, and The Vocal. Each component contributes to the overall success of a presentation.

The Visual

1. Deliver your message in a way that doesn't make the audience feel disrespected or left out. Greet the owners of the establishment, noting the quality of their hospitality for welcoming you in.
2. Be mindful of your body language and facial expressions.

3. People often are not just invested in your work: they might also be invested in how you feel about doing what you're doing. Make sure your body language *accents* the words you say.
4. Stand erect and look confident
5. Pretend there is a camera in front of you when you are on stage. You would not want any shot to come out bad. A confident pose denotes a positive outlook.

The Verbal

1. **Use simple descriptive language.** When writing your own speech, you may be under pressure to find just the right words to say. Pull out a dictionary or thesaurus and keep words in your vocabulary that turn your informal language into words that are more concise, yet still convey the right meaning.
2. **Keep it relatable to your audience**. It is good to make your audience feel welcome in the house, to allow them to sit back and receive what you are saying. Speaking over them, or in words they can't understand, can sometimes offend them, and at other times make the material seem harder to learn.
3. **Don't assume the audience "knows" about your agency or programs**. Catering to "just the regulars" can be bad when you have many people in the audience that perhaps do not know all about the norms of your prior performances. Give a little context or background to your presentation; make it easy for everyone to get on board. This goes with "knowing your audience." Learn about the history of your host and the city of your venue and invite your audience's attention to it, sharing interesting facts your audience might enjoy. Taking time to do research into the history of the host city or venue will undoubtedly be pleasing to the attendees.

THE SKILL OF MAKING YOUR PRESENTATION

The Vocal

1. **Speak "loud and clear".** People in general appreciate any good presenter who knows how to project his voice to be heard in the back of the room. **Use inflection in your voice (volume and pitch).** Not just the words, but every sound counts. Depending on the character you are portraying (if in a play), animation and the way you alter your voice makes you more believable and enjoyable.
2. **Remember to breathe.** Speaking for a long time can tire you out. Take a breather from the delivery of your speech by inserting a bit of comic relief to allow the audience to interact briefly. Such rest can be of help to you and your audience to recuperate from the delivery of a lot of material.

Imagine your Success

Commit as much of your material to memory as possible. This will decrease nervousness and anxiety. Be comfortable when you step in front of your audience. Have a confident positive attitude about what you are about to do. See your audience as involved before you even walk onto the stage. **When you visualize yourself successful, you will increase your confidence in being successful.**

Experience builds confidence, which is key to effective speaking. Start with small groups, or test groups, to gain feedback. Ask family and friends for their opinion to help finalize your delivery.

In summary, a good performance takes being prepared. Preparation is key.

Embracing the Art of Presentation

We've gone over points in this chapter that all sum up to making a thought-provoking, entertaining performance. We have emphasized points about performances that will entertain your audience, whether through your attitude and appearance on stage, your attention to the way you deliver, your volume and rhythm, or through the planned outline of words you've prepared.

Much of the work that goes into making a performance successful is the job of both leader and participants, ensuring the audience and your sponsoring organization are getting the best return on their investment. As we have mentioned, planning and preparation by you and your whole team is key. Those in your organization should come together with the different skills they each offer and be of the same mindset, which is not always easy, but attainable.

This brings us to our final discussion, which ties together the six other themes we have discussed throughout this work: **The Skill of Teamwork.**

Quotes on Making Your Presentation

*No audience ever complained about a
presentation or speech being too short.*
Steven Keague

*Improvement is achieved by the ripple effect of a few simple
changes in approach, attitude or habit.*
Dale Ludwigs

Knowledge is of no value unless you put it into practice.
Anton Chekhov

Scriptures for Making Presentations

*And he said, My presence shall go with thee,
and I will give thee rest.*
Exodus 33:14

*The Lord is on my side; I will not fear:
what can man do unto me?*
Psalm 118:6

*For God hath not given us the spirit of fear;
but of power, and of love, and of a sound mind.*
2 Timothy 1:7

CHAPTER VII:

The Skill of Teamwork

We're stronger together.

Even small actions can have a big impact, when we work together.

President Bill Clinton

Teamwork is:

1. The acting together by a number of people to make the work of the group successful and effective.
2. Cooperative or coordinated effort on the part of a group of persons acting together as a team or in the interests of a common cause.
3. Football teams, baseball teams, basketball teams: these teams all work together, coordinating their effort in harmony to achieve a successful outcome.

The accomplishments that have been discussed in previous chapters could not and would not have been possible without the cooperation and working together of teams. Teamwork was at the core of each life skill implemented. It brought together people with the desire to be part of a team, and in the end produced a product holistically better than what could have been achieved individually. *Teamwork is each component functioning together inter-dependently.* The acting together by a number of people in the GBTAA made the work of the group successful.

> *Make my joy complete by being of the same mind,*
> *maintaining the same love, united in spirit,*
> *intent on one purpose.*
>
> Philippians 2:2

Striving for "Perfection"

Excellence can be obtained when we strive for perfection. When we strive to be excellent, we maintain a standard which is set by the group, and it proves to others they can achieve more than the norm, more than just obtaining satisfactory results. The effort a group puts into effecting change makes the difference between producing average work versus high-quality work. The goal is to strive for perfection with every plan, which yields results that are admirable and true to their mission.

> *Coming together is a beginning; keeping together is progress; working together is success.*
>
> Henry Ford

The process of teamwork is cultivated over time. It involves fostering interactions between people striving towards the same purpose. Let's go over some of these steps one by one.

Step 1: Coming Together

Coming together is one critical lesson to be learned in the experience of working with people. You are halfway to your goal when you reach the point at which your team finally achieves a mutual understanding. On the other hand, avoiding meetings can make your team's mission harder to achieve. Even the most well-thought-out plans that are documented can be difficult when you do not have meetings to communicate your intentions and overall vision.

Step 2: Keeping Together

The more people on the team who are confident in the skills they bring to the process, the more you as a leader can relax in knowing-there are capable people keeping the mission going. It would be hard to fathom this same accomplishment being reached by a one-man show, or a lone ranger.

Step 3: Working Together

One person cannot bring to the table the amount of talent, skills, and creativity many individuals can. A team-oriented task requires the cooperation of multiple people who know what is expected in their roles. Having a dedicated team of contributors, all willing to cooperate and achieve a successful result, is essential regardless of the size of the operation.

> *None of us are as smart as all of us.*
> Japanese proverb, also attributed to Kenneth Hartley Blanchard, American author and management expert.

Productive Meetings

Meetings don't waste time if participants are given action items with deadlines. When participants leave, they should understand the projects to be completed before the next scheduled meeting.

Make attendance at meetings a priority for everybody, regardless of their position. It's not about taking up space in a room; it's about showing a small token of your investment in the group's progress.

The initial meeting is where that first step in judgment takes place. This is the time when people realize, "Yes, this team is worth my investment in time and energy."

Embracing Change

Every leader must adopt an ability to embrace change. However, leaders as well as members must learn to adapt. It will be easier to adapt to change when the attitudes exhibited by your group are aligned with your goals. There are times when attitudes are displayed when one doesn't want to fulfill their obligations. They quickly state "That's not my job and refuse to be a team player." This is displaying a negative attitude and is unacceptable.

It is important for members of a team to accept the possibilities change might bring, even if they do not initially agree.

Equal Responsibility

All who are involved in a team effort, must agree to the commitment and direction of the team and its desired outcome. Whatever the assigned role each member has, it must be performed to the best of one's ability. We must practice an attitude of gratitude and do unto others as you would have them do unto you.

When you miss a meeting, or do not arrive on time, it shifts the atmosphere and focus of the meeting. Being late is an interruption to the meeting involving those already present—it is a distraction and a disturbance. Individuals already seated may have been in the midst of a solemn or a thought-intensive discussion, which you just interrupted. In addition, information you missed might in fact be of help to you and your team in fulfilling your obligations. This includes putting egos aside and receiving instructions, whether leading or following.

It should go without saying that the team leaders should not be late to meetings; as a leader you are to enforce the rules, not disregard them.

Working as the administrator of my church, I witnessed and experienced many challenges because of the limitless responsibilities incurred for all the jobs needing to be fulfilled. At times, there were fewer individuals available than were needed to fill each position, causing many to multi-task. Therefore, the desired outcome and intended success depended highly upon everyone giving their best.

Here are a few starter ideas to help leaders forge ahead:

- Practice an attitude of gratitude.
- Don't take life for granted. Always be appreciative for the blessings you receive.
- Don't expect something for nothing.
- Don't feel privileged or have a sense of entitlement.
- Surround yourself with people who are pleased with and encourage your success

> *We can't become what we need to be by remaining where we are.*
>
> Max de Pree

German-born Eckhart Tolle, world-renowned teacher and author, taught that our ego gets in the way of us living our best life. Oprah Winfrey reinforced his message with a powerful saying,

Through self-acceptance, living in the moment, finding our truths and giving ourselves to a higher purpose, we unleash our best.

I liken this concept to salvation; giving oneself to a higher power will unleash our best. JESUS is the BEST! When we allow Him to be the governing factor in our lives, we unleash nothing but the BEST.

Proper Etiquette and Manners

Additional components of teamwork, in terms of interpersonal (social) skills, are proper etiquette and manners. Etiquette and manners differ depending on the culture. However, they are a part of everyday life and should be encompassed in everything we do. These two skills are of the utmost importance, as they have historically continued to dissipate from one generation to the next.

Etiquette and manners are also necessary in leading a fulfilling and productive life. As you learn to show yourself friendly and be accepting to others' dispositions, you will see the impact in developing proper etiquette and manners. Extending common courtesies and consideration towards others increases your chances of understanding perspectives and making lasting friendships.

Remember, to develop it,
you must use it.

What is proper etiquette and what are manners?

Etiquette: *the customary code of polite behavior in society or among members of a particular profession or group.*

Opening and holding the door for others or taking the coats of guests who enter your home are both examples of proper etiquette. At the dinner table, proper etiquette should always be a requirement, such as knowing which utensil to use and when: dinner fork or salad fork, soup spoon or teaspoon.

Manners: *a way in which a thing is done or happens.* Keeping a polite tone when speaking to others, using please and thank you/I appreciate you, and offering your seat to someone else, are all signs of being well-mannered.

Hospitality: *the quality or disposition of receiving and treating guests and strangers in a warm, friendly, generous way.*

Guests are sure to feel welcome and more comfortable when their needs are met.

When a customer enters a salon, they are greeted by the stylist or receptionist. Your act of acknowledging their presence and making the client feel welcome and at ease, is an example of hospitality.

Precedence: *the order of ceremonial or formal preference.*

The right or need to be dealt with before somebody or something else or to be treated as more important as somebody or something else. Priority.

In situations where two groups of people appear to conflict in established protocol, it is vital for proper order to be openly communicated. For example, in various churches the pastor and visiting clergy take precedence in the funeral procession over the family. The clergy are first escorted to their respective seating, since they will likely conduct the service. Immediately following the clergy, the family members are ushered in, then any remaining guests.

Customer service: *when a group provides customers with assistance or being attentive to what customers are expecting.*

Visiting a church or any other unfamiliar place for the first time can be an unnerving experience. The ushers can potentially relieve some of your anxiety by how they greet you.

Extending their hand, they might say, "Good morning!" "Welcome!" "I'm happy to seat you" "This way please,". These are all great welcoming gestures ushers can use to make visitors feel relaxed and welcome. This is offering customer service.

Happiness adds and multiplies as we divide it with others.
Arthur C. Nielsen

Reaping a Habit

Sow a thought, you reap an *action*. Sow an action, you reap a *habit*. And once you form or develop a *habit*, it becomes second nature, a natural part of you, having been acquired through repetition. Practice, practice, practice until your new *habit* feels comfortable. *Habit* are learned through trial and error, persistence, and commitment.

You can see the power of developing a habit when you look at my experience as a salon owner. Implementing customer service can be very demanding. As the proprietor and executive of "The Grand Barber and Beauty Salon," I made a point of focusing on customer service in every scheduled meeting with my employees. Making customers feel welcome was top priority.

Owning and operating a 28-chair, full-service salon is a massive undertaking to say the least. There were twelve barber chairs in one section. In another section, there were sixteen cosmetology chairs, and manicure stations. Finally, in their own space were the pedicure stations and the massage rooms. It's a business where there is a high turnover of employees, primarily because many cosmetologists/ barbers prefer to work as independent contractors as opposed to employees.

During our meetings, what became a deliberate part of every meeting was to practice our greetings with fellow employees to ensure we greeted customers with a "Good morning," "How can I help you," "Have a seat," or "I'll be with you shortly." If there was a receptionist on duty, they would do the honors, plus the offering of coffee, water, or whatever we had to offer. An employee stated he was very uncomfortable with incorporating customer service in this manner. Having been unaccustomed to performing this service in my newly established business, the Grand Salon, he stated, "I feel weird, phony." (It hadn't become a habit.)

One customer was taken aback at this customer service gesture but accepted with pleasure. I had greeted him then offered him a hot beverage on a chilly morning. Now after 20 years of service—and much tea and coffee—this customer continues to be a dedicated patron at the new establishment, Classic Cuts. And that same employee who was uncomfortable greeting customers now owns his own salon, which he named Classic Cuts

Barber-Shop: The Art of Fine Cutting, where customer service is at the forefront of the business model. And everyone who works there must practice it. According to clients and other visitors, many proclaim, customer service is "off the chain."

At the time of this writing, this employee had built a very successful business that is still growing. He has since told me, "Now I understand! I get it, Mom." Customers need to know you are there for them and be made to feel welcome. As I had instilled this *habit* in him at a young age, he eventually started practicing customer service at the Grand Salon, before starting his own business where this *habit* had become a part of him. You might say today he is a *"Creature of Habit."* Creating or establishing an *effective habit* is now not only a part of his life, but also the lives of others.

> *If you bring your manners, your class, and your dignity to the job, you will do well, along with your knowledge.*
> Bernie Brillstein

Uniting Minds

The teachings received at GBT emphasized that everyone ought to be of the same mind and same intent. The idea of having many minds working together should automatically bring about a sense of unity. When we employed entertainment through the use of performing arts, it became a natural way for us to convey essential material. We used visual aids and attention-grabbing ideas in our own unconventional way.

As the director of these programs, I was committed to creating an impactful experience. This commitment required bringing together the minds of the people to operate in unity, striving to implement the same vision.

Just as the Pastor taught through the Word of God the way we ought to conduct ourselves as parishioners, he showed that an effective administrator takes the initiative to show others the way it's done. Techniques amount to nothing in the absence of both teamwork and team worth. People should be made to feel worthy to be on the team.

This chapter completes the discussion on the seven life skills that aided in cultivating a church's path to greater achievement, with the overall focus being ORGANIZATION. Strive to incorporate these values into your daily life. You will find them very rewarding.

T.E.A.M.

Together

Everyone

Achieves

More

Summary

The main purpose of this book is to propose seven wholesome topics, that will confirm that organization is the umbrella under which all other six life skills are housed. Without organization the other six have no purpose. The term organization means to align business processes into an effective working order. Organization is the foundation out of which order develops. It is a quality that leaders must incorporate into their entire lifestyle, for without it, the techniques used to train on the job, and even one's own personal habits, simply become chaotic. You must have organization.

At each step on this journey, readers must examine themselves to better understand what seeds of administration they already possess, and what seeds they can nurture and improve for their own personal development. In this book I give advice on traits to look for in people showing great potential to one day take the mantle and become leaders themselves. Not one of my life's greatest achievements would have been possible without each one of these skills being embedded into my way of life. Don't be afraid to integrate these life skills into your life—as you begin to see yourself assigned to great projects, rehearse what we've covered in this book as a reminder of how to prosper in your administration.

In the first chapter, **Administration**, we give our first example, and explore a bit of background, helping to explain what is typically expected of leaders and administrators using the history of how administration became a life skill. Being an administrator requires having and continuously developing human, technical, and conceptual skills, in order to convey the methods, techniques, and a sense of competency to their followers.

Life itself is enveloped under an umbrella of organized components, without which we would be overwhelmed by confusion. **Organization** is necessary to move any team forward and toward a common goal. In this chapter we share practical examples of how to effectively execute group gatherings. We elaborate on good organization through numerous examples displaying a variety of large-group events along with the plans that were successfully implemented in anniversaries, weddings, funerals, and group excursions.

The third chapter, **Leadership**, gives more historical context on choices leaders made in various scenarios throughout history. Looking back at leaders whose popularity rose to great prominence in Biblical history, we point out the traits of these leaders, as they are well-worth pondering when anticipating how to become a better leader. Two great stories from my tenure at GBT illustrate how I, along with my coworkers, brought together not just one… but two great projects!!

In the final four chapters, the focus moves to the challenges of implementing leadership. Chapter Four, **Listening**, focuses on skills and wisdom that teach you how to increase your height of awareness among different learning styles. Being a good listener and knowing how to effectively respond to situations is vital to adapting to a new administrative role. Chapter Five, **Communication**, illustrates how administrators can relay new information to their followers, while helping to maintain a healthy two-way conversation. In this chapter, we give three communication strategies, where you'll be sure to find one to suit your message of communication. Chapter Six, **Presentation**, is for those who may not be secure about their ability to present themselves in the spotlight. Here, we summarize well-rehearsed advice that is proven effective for both the leader and follower, learning to strengthen themselves in the fine art of onstage presentation.

Finally, an administrator cannot be effective without maintaining an effective communication link between themselves and their team. We wind-down our story of leadership with the final chapter on **Teamwork**, focusing on the strengths that can be expected of a well-structured team working together to achieve the same goal.

By sowing seeds of hope, these skills brought about a change as we were led down a path to greater achievement. We were led down this path by the life and "life skills" implemented at Greater Beth-el Temple.

If you're in doubt, practice these little pieces of advice until they become a part of you. Learn all you can whether you feel it necessary or not. You never know when it will be needed.

Teamwork Quotes

The achievements of an organization are the results of the combined effort of each individual.
                                        Vince Lombardi

There is no I in team, and there's no I in success either.
                                        Bob Nardelli

No man or woman is an island. To exist just for yourself is meaningless. You can achieve the most satisfaction when you feel related to some greater purpose in life, something greater than yourself.
                                        Denis Waitley

Teamwork Scriptures

For we are labourers together with God: ye are God's husbandry, ye are God's building.
                                        1 Corinthians 3:9

And he gave some, apostles; and some, prophets, and some, evangelists; and some pastors and teachers.
                                        Ephesians 4:11

For the body is not one member but many.
                                        1 Corinthians 12:14

Personal Reflections

Life is but a vapour that appeareth for a little while and then vanisheth away.

James 4:14

With this in mind, take full advantage of the time, and of the gifts and abilities given you by God.

This concludes my discussion with you, in hopes I have unveiled the importance of developing and executing your life skills. It is these skills, which vary from one person to the next, that will carry you to higher heights and deeper depths as you mature and increase in wisdom, understanding, and knowledge.

Your *attitude* determines your *altitude*. What is yours?

However advanced your life skills, there's always room for improvement. Develop an attitude of becoming a lifelong learner and soaking up all life has to offer. Learning is not limited to the classroom only, nor a traditional formal education. You also learn by living. Life itself is one of life's most effective teachers. Learning should be a continual process which enhances understanding of the world we inhabit and improves the quality of our lives.

The formation of this book was prompted by the encouragement of others who saw and believed in my abilities to bring this work to fruition. These individuals urged me to share my story due to the mutual blessings received over the course of our relationships. They hoped that what I could share would positively impact others who desired to improve their own life situations. As a result, and after much deliberation, I decided to share through my story how, when you put God first in your life, He will give you the desires of your heart, and bless you in a measure greater than your highest expectations.

Sometimes, even if you don't recognize them, the countless works you do have unintended outcomes.

I had no intention of gaining any self-satisfaction by completing this body of work nor, — not even an inkling — of this work becoming a part of my own life's journey. My story and the information I've shared began as a mere thought – a dim light in the corner of my mind. This thought ultimately gave way to the idea of implementing in print what I'd learned and practiced over the past 40 years of service and, in the administrative positions I've held.

Throughout those many years, I've learned, without a doubt, that to successfully work together, being organized is crucial. Collaborating with different mindsets, backgrounds, customs, and the like takes a combined effort on everyone's part, as gifts vary from person to person. We complement each other's abilities with our unique strengths and weaknesses; in so doing we complete each other.

> *An organized team makes an individual's*
> ***good**, **better**...and the teams **better** becomes*
> *the outcome's **best**!*
>
> Randy J. Goodwin

From an early age, the process of becoming organized has stirred within me. As far back as I can remember, finding ways to make life a bit easier to manage became somewhat an obsession of mine. I would ask myself, "What can I do to make my life and the lives of others more peaceable, enjoyable, and less stressful?"

Making myself available and attempting to lighten the load for my family was the beginning. As the eldest of three siblings and being raised, on a farm in extreme poverty conditions, I was expected to assist and even manage the day-to-day responsibilities of the home inside and out. My duties inside consisted of cooking and cleaning for the entire family, which (at times) included, my Mother, sister, brother, uncles, Grandmother, and Grandfather, with whom I had lived for an extended portion of my young life. Some outdoor duties included the cutting of firewood for heating and cooking, and the feeding and care of all animals.

I also worked in the agricultural arena (farming). In those days, families raised and harvested nearly all food that grew up from the ground. Much love and care were given to how the seedlings and plants were handled while they grew and matured, as they would provide the essential minerals and nutrients necessary for our livelihood. The rewards reaped and the results of observing how God caused these plants to materialize caused me to ponder in amazement.

Another area I was required to labor in, was the raising of cotton. I not only chopped cotton, I picked and pulled it as well. At the age of ten, I could pick 200 lbs. of cotton per day, and at age fifteen, I was picking 300 lbs. For 12 hours of work, at the rate of $2.50 and $3.00 per 100 lbs. of cotton, I earned seven to nine dollars per day in total. Hard to believe? Looking back, it's even hard for me to believe.

I accepted whatever fell my lot without murmuring and complaining, because I was keenly aware of the need and wanted to assist in fulfilling that need. Even in my youth, I applied the skills and talents God gifted me as I continued to grow in stature, and in wisdom, understanding, and knowledge.

In my mid-twenties, my life ultimately took a different turn, thrusting me into a place that progressively shaped my adult life. This direction provided me a foundation and structure to embark upon, in my newly appointed position as administrator of my church. To God be the glory for all I've experienced throughout that 40 years of my life, spent at Greater Bethel Temple: the knowledge gained, the expansion of my gifts, and the skills I was able to apply. I am so thankful for this rare opportunity to share some of these morsels with you.

As stated in the scripture, I firmly believe that *all things work together for good to them who love God—to them who are the called according to his purpose.* (Romans 8:28)

Strive to serve the Lord with gladness, maintaining a positive attitude of perseverance, *'acknowledging always the author and finisher of our faith,' 'For God is not unrighteous to forget your work and labor of love,' 'as he is a rewarder of them that diligently seek him.'* (Hebrews 12:2; 6:10; 11:6)

"But by the grace of God I am what I am: and his grace which was bestowed upon me was not in vain; but I laboured more abundantly than they all: yet not I, but the grace of God which was with me." (1 Corinthians 15:10)

Acknowledgments

To the members of my Greater Beth-el Temple family in Christ, who assisted me with this immense undertaking through life's invaluable lessons (including my assistants: La Ronda (Donaldson) Birch, Nancy L. Clute, Rita Mae Dantzler, Ernestine (Peak) Hawkins, Donna M. Miller, Ella Mae Tisdel; and my junior assistants: Jeanette Fairchild, Teia D. (Blair) Goodwin, Deborah L. (Clute) Petru, Angel N. Starks.

Your priceless contributions, through kindness, patience, and loyalty, have not gone unobserved; in fact, your charities are glaringly rich!

For many years, you abetted me with your generosity and loving-kindness, to which I am indebted with thanks and gratitude. Your faith, hope and love helped to guide us through any undertaking we envisioned. Without charity (love) orchestrated throughout our time together, we would have only been as "sounding brass or a tinkling cymbal." (1 Corinthians 13:1)

There are many irreplaceable individuals who have impacted my life in countless ways, to whom I wish to express my sincere gratitude.

To My Five Sons:

I want to extend a heartfelt thank you to my sons Kevin D., Bryon E., Randy J., Darian L., and David E. Goodwin Jr, and to my two daughters-in-law, Yvette M. and Tunese A. ("Coco"). It has been rewarding watching you develop into accomplished adults. Without your assistance and untiring labor of love, reaching this milestone in my life would not have been nearly as achievable if not impossible. I feel a sense of pride when I reflect on the years spent perfecting the many performances you willingly and sometimes unwillingly participated, but you persevered, culminating in a product well worth your investment. You make my heart glad!

To Judith Fairchild-Wells:

From the onset of my newly appointed position, you assisted whenever needed. Your secretarial skills were "just what the Doctor ordered." You prompted my first official church recognition through the Young People's Auxiliary for the formation of the Junior Pastor's Aide committee, which taught young people how to work in church. I will always be grateful for your kindness during those formative years.

To David Anthony Clute:

In the continuation of my appointed positions, and after your coming of age, you willingly donated your time whether day or night. We struggled and sacrificed regardless of the hour, making sure our timelines were met. You encouraged, gave suggestions, and continued to support my many endeavors, initiating the completion of my post-graduate education. You are seriously appreciated.

To Deborah L. (Clute) Petru:

My "daughter by another mother": for your invaluable commitment to this material, and for your skill, compassion, and loyalty—not only in your devotion to this work, but moreover for your unyielding faith as a dedicated assistant for the many years we've spent together. The Lord shall not forget your labor of love, and neither shall I.

To Lorraine McCroy-Griffin:

"To make a long story short," your relentless encouragement throughout the years has been an incessant source of strength. Your belief in my abilities to make this vision a reality long before I ever thought it possible, is appreciated beyond the words on this page.

To Dr. Ronald W. Alston, Sr.

I take great inspiration and advice from you, particularly as an accomplished author and lecturer. (drronalston.com). You insisted my story needed to be on paper, especially for the benefit of my sons and their families. Your persistent prodding and coaching was a major catalyst that gave me the courage to bring this desire to completion. I am truly grateful for the timing of our friendship.

To Rudy and Allana Smith:

You were the initiators of my first-ever community awards received outside of GBT, the first being the *2008 Woman of Color Award* from the University of Nebraska at Omaha, the second being the 2010 Black History Month Honoree (read into Congressional Record by Nebraska Congressman Lee Terry), both of which are mentioned in this volume of work. You were surely used by God to bestow upon me mounds of support and blessings, extending beyond my wildest dreams. The crossing of our paths is a moment I will forever cherish.

In memory of Dr. Dura Hale (d. 2012)

You initiated the community outreach of the GBT Academy of the Arts, by providing the opportunity to perform for the legendary Tuskegee Airmen in honor of their service to our country during World War II. Thank you for your belief in me and the Academy's mission to coordinate such grand event in Milwaukee, WI. Sharing your vision to carry on the legacy of these brave men through our collaboration with MAAST (Milwaukee Academy of Aviation, Science and Technology) was awe-inspiring.

In memory of Bishop McArthur Anderson (d. 2016)

My brother in the gospel, and strong initiator behind this book. You never ceased to call me in the wee hours of the morning, inspiring me to move forward in sharing the administrative skills God gifted me. You believed in my abilities, and through the use of scripture, faithfully encouraged me that I could 'do all things through Christ, which strengthens me,' and that 'God shall not forget my labor of love.' (Philippians 4:13; Hebrews 6:10)

(During the writing of this book, Bishop Anderson transitioned from this life to Glory.)

He would be delightfully satisfied to know this book is no longer a Vision, it has become a Reality; thanks to his unwavering determination for me to always "B BOUT IT!" (Be About It!)

NOW as our lives move on, three things remain:
Faith, Hope, and Love.
HOWEVER, the greatest of these is Love...
I thank you for yours.

My acknowledgments would not be complete if these individuals were not included:

Teia Goodwin, I'm appreciative for your efforts, and for encouraging me to take the plunge.

Jonathan Saddler, my contributing editor and star grammar student—and with many other words did you exhort saying, "C'mon Dr. C, let's do this!" Thank you for going the distance with me.

Patricia Starr, author of *Angel on my Handlebars* and joint-author of *The Unstoppable Entrepreneur*: I appreciate the time you sacrificed to proofread my work, and for your positive influence during the time we spent together working toward a common goal.

Thank you all for your recommendations,
your helpful corrections and suggestions in the
compilation of this book.

Thought Expansion

Results of Teamwork Demonstrated

The outcome of every Auxiliary's work proved to be successful with the implementation of these seven life skills.

The Choir received unanimous praise locally and nationally for its uniformity, harmony, presentation of songs, and the positive response from the audience was encouraging when lifting their voices in praise.

The Usher Board obtained higher levels of professionalism with exceptional care given to escorting and seating of guests. They effectively exhibited the preferred manner of dress and modeled first-rate customer service.

The Brotherhood taught brothers how to be men in business, and in handling of secular matters, allowing the Pastor his own time to tend to the flock by studying and teaching the word of God.

The Young People's activities proved they were effective in their presentations by how their programs energized both the congregation and the youth themselves. The Young People provided educational programs that afforded them new opportunities and experiences abroad.

The Pastor's Aide auxiliary shouldered responsibilities within the church in support of its foundational principles, lifting up the congregation with them. They lightened the load and burdens, by working diligently with the man of God to enable him to fulfill his pastoral duties more effectively.

The Missionary Auxiliary taught the young women how to prepare their lives for womanhood, covering a wide range of topics including housekeeping, child-rearing, and marriage. These topics were very enlightening not just to the young women, but the more mature also. We are never too old to gain wisdom, understanding, and knowledge; this should be our attitude.

The Sunday School also improved its planning and organizational practices by developing a more impactful curriculum that merged relatable topics from our secular lives with Biblical truths. The teachers carefully tailored lessons applicable to each age group.

> *Through teamwork, ordinary people can achieve extraordinary results. We all do better when we all do better.*

Goal Oriented Teamwork

This display of names lists the auxiliaries and committees with whom I worked during those many years at GBT.

Administrative Offices -Donna D.
Alter Workers/Tarrying Team- Johnny W.
Audio/Visual Nichole W.
Brotherhood Eld. LD M.
Combined Choirs Tunese G.
Deacons Edward D.
Decorations Shirlene N.
Junior Brotherhood Bryce D.
Junior Missionary Shannel D.
Junior Pastors Aide Elois S.
Missionary Linda L.
Mothers Club Valery G.
Nurses Guild- Ella M. T.
Pastors--Aide Rita M.D.
Pastors Office- Donna M.
Pastors Table Donna M.
Publication Gwendolyn G.
Sunday School Dr. William C.
Usher Board/Hospitality Dec. Gerald L. Elois S.
Weddings and Funerals Laronda B.
Young People Elder Calvin G. Sr.

Photo Gallery A

The following illustrations are but a small representation of the table settings arranged and decorated by the talented members of the Greater Beth-el Temple and GBT Academy of the Arts. The coming together of these table settings demonstrates the essence of all seven life skills.

- The **Leadership** of the pastor's table chairlady.
- The planning out of each detail, and proper **administration** of jobs.
- How the committee members **listened** to the vision, which was then executed by all.
- The **teamwork** of all involved working at their best on their part.
- **Communicating** the vision through their designs.
- The **presentation** of each element in its rightful place in the display.
- And bringing it all together under the umbrella of **organization**.

PHOTO GALLERY A

PHOTO GALLERY A

Well done is better than well said.
Benjamin Franklin

APPENDIX A:

Photo Gallery B

The following images represent but a fraction of the work mentioned in this body of work during my tenure as Administrator of Greater Beth-el Temple and Executive Producer-Director of GBT Academy of the Arts (GBTAA).

Dr. C presented with Directors chair following a program at Embassy Suites Hotel

Private Collections by (MJ) Dr. C

Dr. C (MJ) taking care of business during the grand opening of the Grand Barber & Beauty Salon

Grand opening of the Grand Barber & Beauty Salon

Barbers taking care of business on opening day

Dr. C's Assistants (from left to right): Rita Dantzler, Yvette Goodwin & LaRonda Birch, in front of 30x5 ft. mural of North 24th St created by GBTAA artists

GBTAA Mural Artists from left to right: Debbie (Clute) Petru, Teonne (Daye) Clark, Maurice Patterson, Yvette Goodwin (lead artist), Shirlene Nicholson

GBTAA Honor Guard, following a special tribute in Des Moines, IA

GBTAA Jazz Band, actor Meshach Taylor (center) following Black History performance at University of Nebraska at Omaha

GBTAA Jazz Band with actor Obba Babatunde (center) and Dr. C. following "Through the Fire" performance at University of Nebraska at Omaha

Dr. C. presenting the book, "Black Genius," at a Black History celebration

GBTAA Interpretive Dancers following an 80th birthday celebration performance

From left to right: Natalie Carter, Marcella Dial, Candace Gould, Dr. C, Yvette Goodwin, Tunese Goodwin, Debbie (Clute) Petru

GBTAA rendition of Branson's Shoji Tabuchi and the Milk Cow Blues performance. Fiddler Bryon Goodwin, Three cows are Teia Goodwin, Dorothea Clute, Marcella Dial costumes designed and created by artist Yvette Goodwin

Dressed for visit to White House Garden initiated by First Lady Michelle Obama. From left to right (top row): Nancy Clute, Tunese Goodwin, Dr. C., Bessie Ebow (bottom row) Lorraine Coleman, Debbie (Clute) Petru, Rita Dantzler.

These two photos are all the same individuals. Dr. C. and team on their way to Washington, D.C. after Dr. C. received Congressional honor tribute.

Dr. C and Dr. Dura Hale, a graduate of Tuskegee University, Dr. Hale initiated the celebration of the legendary Tuskegee Airmen bi-annually in Milwaukee, Wisconsin

Dr. C and Col. Charles McGee following GBTAA Tribute to the legendary Tuskegee Airmen in Milwaukee, Wisconsin

GBTAA Honor Guard performing in honor of Tuskegee Airmen (Red Tails) in Milwaukee, Wisconsin

Five of 21 Tuskegee Airmen Honorees

GBTAA Honor Guard with General Benjamin O. Davis, impersonated by actor Randy J. Goodwin

Black History Presentation GBTAA opening for Dr. Bernard & Shirley Kinsey at the Nate Holden Performing Arts Center in Los Angeles, California

Dr. C receiving Congressional Honor from Nebraska Congressman Lee Terry during Black History Month 2010

Dr. C meeting Fox News anchor Kelly Wright, which later resulted in a news story covering the GBTAA Academy.

Dr. C with Lance R. Foster II, a GBTAA protégé and Secret Service Agent, under President Barrack Obama's administration

Dr. C during Greater Beth-el Temple's Celebration of Legends, adapted from Oprah Winfrey's Legends Ball.

Author and renowned speaker, Dr. Michael Eric Dyson, with Dr. C and Academy members at UNO

Dr. C and Academy members with B. Smith and husband, Dan Gasby, at their Washington, D.C. restaurant

Dancers following a Hawaiian inspired performance

Trip to Branson, MO, boarding for excursion on the Showboat Branson Belle

Re-enactment of Michael Jackson tribute.

Costumes designed by Academy members.

Chicken Dance performance by GBTAA Kitty Kats

"Through the Fire" GBTAA Fundraiser performance by Kitty Kats at UNO (Dorothy the good witch impersonation) by Dorothea Clute, center

Woodmen of the World Honor Plaque

Presented by Exec. Vice Pres. of Finance and Treasurer Mark L. Schreier with wife Diana, Olivia Crimniel-Minor and Rita Dantzler receiving Honor Plaque for Dr. C

APPENDIX B:

Inspirational Passages

First, it is an intention.
Then a behavior.
Then a habit.
Then a practice.
Then a second nature.
Then it is simply who you are.

— Brendon Burchard

QUOTES ON WISDOM AND KNOWLEDGE

Wisdom is not a product of schooling,
but of the lifelong attempt to acquire it.
— Albert Einstein

Knowledge, you may get from books, but Wisdom
is trapped within you, release it.
— Ismat Ahmed Shaikeh

Men must be taught as if you taught them not, and things
unknown proposed as things forgot.
— Alexander Pope

SCRIPTURES ON WISDOM AND KNOWLEDGE

If any of you lack wisdom, let him ask of God,
that giveth to all men liberally, and upbraideth not;
and it shall be given him.
— James 1:5

The fear of the Lord is the beginning of wisdom: a good
understanding have all they that do his commandments: his
praise endureth forever.
— Psalms 111:10

For wisdom is a defence, and money is a defence: but the
excellency of knowledge is, that wisdom giveth life to them
that have it.
— Ecclesiastes 7:12

APPENDIX C:

Author Publications

Other works in which the author has produced, initiated, planned, or participated:

Implementing the Mind of the Pastor in the Church

Feed My Lambs: An Introduction to Church Government

25th Anniversary Book (the reprinted/revised edition)

The Love Book by Bishop Dr. Nelson G. Turner

APPENDIX D:

Suggested Readings

- **The Bible.** Number one best-seller, but least-read. Everything we need pertaining to life is in the volume of this book. Please note: **All scriptures throughout this publication was taken from the King James Version unless otherwise noted.**
- **You Learn by Living:** Eleanor Roosevelt. Eleven Keys for A More Fulfilling Life. Written by a woman with much wisdom and knowledge who suggest learning extends far beyond the class room. The wife of Franklin D. Roosevelt the 32nd United States President.
- **The Kinsey Collection:** Dr. Bernard and Shirley Kinsey, a couple who collected and conducted extensive research on the history and contributions by African Americans to this great nation. (http://thekinseycollection.com)
- **My Words Your Reality:** Dr. Ron W. Alston. "Your Guide to Personal & Professional Development"
- **"Simply, Common "Cents": The Discipline of Uncommon Reasoning:** Dr. Ron W. Alston. (http://drronalston.com)

- **Gifted Hands:** Dr. Ben Carson. This physician truly personifies the title, "Gifted Hands." He overcame tremendous obstacles from youth to adulthood, his life story being a testament to how strong God can intervene in someone's life and bring out the best in man. He successfully separated conjoined twins connected at the back of the head. By his own admission, such feats could have only come to fruition through his trust in God and relentless belief in his own capabilities.

Index

A

accepting constructive criticism, 127
actively seeking to understand, 170
actors
    identifying, 73, 76
additional learning styles, 149
administration
    scriptures on, 66
    the skill of, 35, 37
administrative skills
    improving, 64
administrator
    what is, 38
animating your audience, 171
announcers, 108
appropriate words, 163
art of presentation, 182
asking clarifying questions, 165
asking questions, 144
assessing your listening behavior, 142
assistant choir directors, 107
associate choir director (finance), 107
associate choir director (robes), 107
Assuming a leadership role, 51
audience
    animating your, 171
auditory learners, 147
auxiliary
    organizing your, 60

B

bible notebooks, 97
body language, 151, 160
brainstorming sessions, 73
breaking into subcommittees, 73, 75
brotherhood auxiliary, 211
business plan, 61

C

candy sales, 99
carryout dinners, 101
change
    embracing, 189
characters and actors
    identifying, 73, 76
choir, 216
    developing leadership, 108
    organizing the, 105
choir directors, 107
choosing
    leaders, 126
clarifying questions, 165
clear and concise messages, 163
coming together, 187
communicating
    assertively, 159
communication
    basics of, 155
    quotes on, 167
    scriptures, 168
    the skill of, 155
communication method, 164
communication strategies, 161
    actively seeking to understand, 170
    asking clarifying questions, 165
    consider diversity factors, 164
    effective listening skills, 165
    recognize disruptive factors, 162
    sending clear and concise messages, 163
    supportive, nonverbal cues, 163
    the appropriate words, 163
    the communication method, 164
    thoroughly understanding communication process, 161
    three effective, 161
conceptual skill, 45
consignment shop, 99

coordinating group travel, 78
creative consultants, 108
criticism
   giving and accepting constructive, 127
customer service, 193
Cutler, Alan, 121

D

dependent person, 48
destinations, 83
determining key scripture, 75
determining key scripture and general program format, 75
determining program format, 75
developing leadership in the choir, 108
diet, 82
director
   associate director (finance), 107
   associate director (robes), 107
   business affairs, 107
   choir director, 107
   executive, 105-106, 109
   lead choir, 106
   minister of music/lead organist, 107
   section leader, 106
director of business affairs, 107
diversity factors, 164

E

editing a script, 76
embracing change, 189
embracing the art of presentation, 182
enhancing teaching methods, 56
equal responsibility, 189
etiquette, 191
executive director, 105-106, 109

F

film festivals, 98
final presentation, 78
fine-tuning a performance, 77
former Greater Beth-el Temple renovation, 133
forming a planning committee, 73
fundraisers
   bible notebooks, 98
   candy sales, 99
   carryout dinners, 101
   film festivals, 98
   holiday bake sales, 99
   nearly new and consignment shop, 99
   planning, 97
   waiter/waitress services, 100
funerals, 104

G

giving constructive criticism, 127
goals
   short and long term, 62
goodwill presentations, 176
Goodwin, Randy J., 171
Greater Beth-el Temple and GBT Children's Academy
   destinations visited, 83
   programs/themes, 74
   sample destination itinerary, 87
group travel
   coordinating, 78
   destinations, 83
   diet, 82
   itinerary, 80, 84-85
   organized packing, 80
   personal hygiene, 82
   pre-trip meeting, 79
   restroom breaks, 83
   snacks, 81, 83

H

habit
   reaping a, 193
healthy and unhealthy stress, 60

INDEX

hearing
    quotes on, 153
    scriptures, 154
holiday bake sales, 99
hospitality, 192, 213
human skill, 40
hygiene
    personal, 82

I

identifying characters and actors, 73, 76
imagine your success, 181
implementing organization, 68
implementing your leader's mind, 54
improving your administrative skills, 64
incorporating creativity, 174
independent person, 48
inspired teaching, 63
inter-dependent person, 48
itinerary, 80, 84-85

K

Katz, Robert L., 38, 40
keeping together, 188
key scripture
    determining, 75
knowledge
    quotes on, 242
    scriptures, 242

L

language
    body, 160, 172
lead choir director, 106, 110
lead organist, 107
leader
    list of characteristics/attributes, 121, 126
    qualities of an effective, 63
leaders
    as mediators, 130
    preparation of, 128
    stepping up, 137
leadership
    choir, 108
    jigsaw, 121
    list of goal-oriented skills, 109
    preparation for greatness, 130
    quotes on, 139
    scriptures, 140
    servant-based, 55
    skill of leadership, 121, 123
leadership scriptures, 140
learning styles, 56, 146
    auditory, 147
    logical, 149
    social, 149
    solitary, 149
    tactile, 148
    verbal, 149
    visual, 146
learning to
    communicate assertively, 159
    listen responsively, 150
    say no, 116
list of
    attributes of leader, 121
    attributes of servants, 56
    characteristics of strong leadership, 121
    goal-oriented leadership skills, 109
    presentation pointers, 3 V's, 179
    presentation pointers, general, 172
    tips for team leaders, 190
listen
    stop, look and, 160
listening
    assessing your listening behavior, 142
    effective listening skills, 165
    quotes on, 153
    responsively, 150
    scriptures, 154
    the skill of listening, 138, 141
listening not the same as hearing, 142
logical learners, 149

M

making a connection, 166
making your presentation
  quotes on, 183
  scriptures, 183
  skill of, 169, 173
making your to-do list, 114
managing your time, 111
managing administrative stress, 59
manners, 191, 192
mediators, 130
meetings
  pre-trip, 79
messages
  clear and concise, 163
  nonverbal, 151
minds
  uniting, 195
minister of music, 107
mission statement, 61
missionary auxiliary, 212
musicians, 107

N

nearly new and consignment shop, 99
new Greater Beth-el Temple
  restoration, 134
no
  saying no, 116
nonverbal cues, 163
nonverbal messages, 151

O

organist, 107
organization
  in the home, 70
  packing, 80
  the skill of, 65, 67
organizational structure
  building an, 61
  of choir, 105
organize
  why, 70

organized packing, 80
organizing
  auxiliary, 61
  choir, 105
  quotes on, 120
  scriptures, 120
organizing the choir, 105
  announcers, 108
  assistant choir directors, 107
  associate choir director (finance), 107
  choir directors, 106
  creative consultants, 108
  director of business affairs, 107
  executive director, 105, 106, 109
  lead choir director, 106, 107, 110
  minister of music/lead organist, 107
  musicians, 107
  organist, 107
  section leaders, 106
outcomes
  final presentation, 78

P

packing for a trip, 80
pastor's aide auxiliary, 212
people skill, 40
perceptions on
  implementing organization, 68
perceptions on implementing
  organization, 68
perfection
  striving for, 187
performance
  rehearsing, 73, 77
personal hygiene, 82
planning
  committee, 73
  funerals, 104
  quotes on, 120
  scriptures, 120
  weddings, 102
  why plan, 72
planning committee
  forming a, 73

planning fundraisers, 97
planning/organizing scriptures, 120
precedence, 192
preparation
    meanings, 128
preparation of leaders, 128
preparing your presentation, 172
presentation
    goodwill, 176
    preparing, 172
    quotes on, 183
    scriptures, 183
    set-ups, 174
    skill of making your, 166, 169
pre-trip meeting, 79
productive meetings, 188
program format
    determining, 75
proper etiquette and manners, 191
    customer service, 193
    etiquette, 191
    hospitality, 192, 213
    manners, 191
    precedence, 192
punctuality, 119

Q

qualities of effective leader, 63
quotes
    leadership, 139
quotes on
communication, 167
listening and hearing, 153
making your presentation, 183
planning/organizing, 120
teamwork, 200
wisdom and knowledge, 242

R

raising children, 114
reaping a habit, 193
recognize disruptive factors, 162

rehearsing a performance, 73, 77
renovation
    new greater Beth-el Temple, 134
responsive listening, 151
restoration
    new greater Beth-el Temple, 134
restroom breaks, 83
results of teamwork demonstrated, 211
    brotherhood auxiliary, 211
    choir, 211
    missionary auxiliary, 212
    pastor's aide auxiliary, 212
    Sunday school auxiliary, 212
    usher board auxiliary, 211
    young people's auxiliary, 212
rewriting a script, 76

S

script
    rewriting, editing and revising, 76
scriptures
    administration, 66
    communication, 168
    leadership, 140
    listening and hearing, 154
    making your presentation, 183
    planning/organizing, 120
    teamwork, 200
    wisdom and knowledge, 242
scriptures on communication, 168
scriptures on listening/hearing, 154
scriptures on making presentations, 183
scriptures on teamwork, 200
scriptures on wisdom and knowledge, 242
section leaders, 106
self-discipline, 117
self-improvement sessions, 177
sending clear and concise messages, 163
service
    customer service, 193

session
   brainstorming, 73
   self-improvement, 177
   training, 176
setting clear expectations, 57
set-ups
   for presentations, 174
short and long term goals, 62
skill
   conceptual, 45
   effective listening skills, 165
   of leadership, 121, 123
   of listening, 138, 141
   making a presentation, 176, 169
   of teamwork, 182, 185
   people/human, 40
   technical, 49
skill of
   administration, 35, 37
   communication, 155
   organization, 65, 67
snacks, 80, 83
social learners, 149
solitary learners, 149
speech
   the spoken word, 157
   writing your, 177
speechwriting, 177
spoken word, 157
stress
   healthy and unhealthy, 60
   managing, 59
striving for perfection, 187
striving for punctuality, 119
subcommittees
breaking into, 75, 77
Sunday school auxiliary, 212
supportive, nonverbal cues, 163

T

tactile learners, 148
teaching
   inspired, 63

teaching children, 114
teamwork
   quotes on, 200
   scriptures, 200
   skill of, 182, 185
   what is, 186
technical skill, 49
thinking outside the box, 178
three effective communication
   strategies, 161
three v's for presentation, 179
time management, 111
to-do list, 114
train up a child, 113
training sessions, 176

U

uniting minds, 195
usher board auxiliary, 211

V

verbal learners, 149
visual learners, 146

W

waiter/waitress services, 100
weddings, 102
wisdom
quotes on, 242
scriptures, 242
word
   spoken, 157
   written, 156
work begins with you, 124
working together, 188
writing a script, 76
writing your speech, 177
written word, 156

Y

young people's auxiliary, 212

Index of Quotations

Ali, Muhammad, 139
Allen, James, 118
Baldwin, James A., 153
Blanchard, Kenneth Hartley, 188
Brillstein, Bernie, 195
Browne, Harry, 119
Burchard, Brennan, 56
Carnegie, Dale, 139
Chekov, Anton, 183
Clinton, Bill, 185
Cushing, Richard, 120
de Pree, Max, 190
Einstein, Albert, 242
Ford, Henry, 187
Getty, J. Paul, 117
Giblin, Les, 170
Goodwin, Randy J., 202
Gracian, Baltazar, 112
Groeschel, Craig, 37
Gunn, Robin Jones, 70
Hubbard, Elbert, 113
Jefferson, Thomas, 50
Judd, Stanley, 120
Keague, Steven, 183
Kelly, Vista M., 139
Kennedy, John Fitzgerald, 39
King, Larry, 153
Lakein, Alan, 120
Larsen, Doug, 153
Lombardi, Vince, 200
Ludwigs, Dale, 183
Maxwell, John C., 125
Nader, Ralph, 123
Nardelli, Bob, 200
Penney, James Cash, 153
Plato, 167
Pope, Alexander, 242
Powell, Lawrence Clark, 167
Powell, Robert Baden, 153
Rawls, Lou, 167
Rosenfeld, Irene, 57
Shaikeh, Ismat Ahmed, 242
Tracy, Brian, 167
Truman, Harry S., 123
Turner, Dale, 66
Waitley, Denis, 200
Washington, Booker T., 66
Winfrey, Oprah, 119, 190
Winston, Bill, 117

www.ingramcontent.com/pod-product-compliance
Lightning Source LLC
Chambersburg PA
CBHW031315160426
43196CB00007B/549